Career Design on DVD

プロフェッショナルに学ぶキャリアデザイン

Kayoko Shiomi

Angus McGregor

Naohiro Takita

Career Design on DVD

Top Careers in Two Years
Business, Finance, and Government Administration

Copyright © 2007 by Infobase Publishing, Inc.

Copyright © 2000 by Facts on File, Inc. Publish under license from Facts On File, Inc, New York

Copyright © 2014 by Kayoko Shiomi, Angus McGregor, Naohiro Takita

All rights reserved for Japan.
No part of this book may be reproduced in any form
without permission from Seibido Co., Ltd.

はじめに

　本書は、DVDを観ながらさまざまな職業について仕事の内容や情報を得ることができる総合教材です。さまざまな分野で働くプロフェッショナルの声から、各分野で求められる技能と資質、および仕事で経験する問題や対処方法、やり甲斐について知ることができます。また、就職前に身につけておくべき知識やスキル、就職に向けての準備の仕方なども、実際に現場で働いている経験者たちから学ぶことができます。

　子供の頃、将来の夢として抱いていた職業のイメージは、漠然としたものだったかもしれません。しかし、大学生になると、卒業後の進路を具体的に考え始めなければなりません。今後ますます進むグローバル社会においては、働く場所は日本国内に留まりません。海外も視野にいれたキャリア形成を考える時代となっています。国際舞台で働くためには、世界から発信される情報を把握すると同時に、自らが情報やアイデアを発信する英語力が必要不可欠になります。

　本書は、世界で活躍できる学生の人材育成を念頭に置き、キャリアデザインと英語学習を融合させた教材です。本書に取り上げるキャリアは15分野の職業で、広報担当者、広告販売者、商品マネージャー、マーケティングマネージャー、オフィスマネージャー、スポーツ＆フィットネスマネージャー、ファッションデザイナー、レクリエーションワーカー、保育園教師、ホテルマネージャー、インテリアデザイナー、ビデオ編集者、DTP出版者、イベントプランナー、写真家と多岐に渡ります。

　本書を学習教材として用いることで、学習者が英語の受信と発信技能を高めると同時に、自分自身のキャリアデザインを考える機会を持つことができれば幸いです。

本書の特徴

①15分野の職業の中身を英語で学ぶことのできるDVD教材。自主学習用DVD付き。
②英語の4技能を高めると同時に、キャリアアドバイスを提供する総合教材。
③各課は6ページで構成され、半期でも通年でも使用可。
④DVDを用いて、英語による情報受信力と同時に発信力を養成。
⑤各分野の仕事の内容と仕事に必要なスキルや準備について学習。
⑥トップダウンとボトムアップリスニングの練習が可能。
⑦サマリーとシャドーイング、およびスピーキングに音声CDあり。
⑧各キャリアに必要な条件やアドバイスを掲載。

本書各 Unit の構成

(1) 各登場者の簡単な仕事内容の説明
(2) Vocabulary
(3) DVD の視聴
　　First Viewing：キャリア概要の把握
　　Second Viewing：聞き取りと書き取り練習
　　Third Viewing：重点項目のメモ取り練習
(4) Comprehension（True/False 問題）
(5) Summary & Shadowing Practice
(6) Sentence Structure（文法選択肢、文法誤用問題、文の並び替え）
(8) Speaking Practice
(9) Activity（Research & Presentation, Role play Interview, Creative Activity）
(10) Career Tips

　なお、(9)のアクティビティセクションはオプショナルで、クラスの時間に合わせて活用してください。アクティビティを通して、学習者は各自調べたことを基にショートスピーチや発表、ロールプレイのインタビュー、あるいはクリエイティブなタスクを行なうことにより、英語の発信力を養成することができます。

　学生がこれからのキャリアを構想していく上で、本書の内容が少しでも役立つことを願っています。

　最後に、本書を作成するにあたり数々のご助言をいただきました成美堂の菅野英一氏と松本健治氏に心より感謝いたします。

著　者

Contents

Unit		語数	DVDの長さ	頁数
1.	**PR Specialist** チームとファンを結ぶ広報宣伝活動	224	1'35"	1
2.	**Advertising Sales Agent** 顧客のニーズを喚起する広告制作と販売促進	312	1'54"	7
3.	**Merchandise Manager** 世界の優れた商品や情報を消費者へ提供	296	1'28"	13
4.	**Marketing Manager** 市場調査と分析に基づいたキャンペーン戦略	276	1'23"	19
5.	**Office Manager** 会社の全体像を見据えたオフィスマネジメント	387	2'32"	25
6.	**Sports and Fitness Manager** 健康作りとエクササイズの支援	328	2'20"	31
7.	**Fashion Designer** 斬新なセンスで創造するファッションデザイン	358	1'43"	37
8.	**Recreation Worker** 心と体を癒すレクリエーション	342	2'05"	43
9.	**Pre-School Teacher** 温かい眼差しで育む幼児の成長	379	2'00"	49
10.	**Hotel Manager** おもてなしの心を込めた提供をするホテルサービス	287	1'37"	55
11.	**Interior Designer** 快適でおしゃれな空間の設計	460	2'25"	61
12.	**Video Editor** 作品の完成度を高める映像編集	482	2'41"	67
13.	**Desktop Publishing** 読みやすく視覚に訴える卓上出版	464	2'29"	73
14.	**Event Planner** 多彩なイベントをプロデュース	561	2'29"	79
15.	**Photographer** 人生の大切な節目を記録に残す写真	419	2'43"	85

Unit 1 PR Specialist

PR スペシャリスト

広報の主な仕事は、企業の活動や業務内容を社内報にまとめて報告したり、さまざまなお知らせや取り組み、イベントなどを新聞や雑誌、ラジオやテレビ、インターネットなどのメディアを使って多くの人に伝わるようにすることです。ここではスポーツ、特に野球チームの広報担当者 Bill Cook 氏に PR の仕事の内容を聞いていきます。

Vocabulary: Match the following English with its Japanese definition.

1. director   (   )   6. vary   (   )
2. public relations (   )   7. critical   (   )
3. entail   (   )   8. résumé   (   )
4. deal with   (   )   9. stick with   (   )
5. brochure   (   )   10. eventually   (   )

a. 典型的な	b. 変わる・異なる	c. 対処する	d. 重要な
e. 会長	f. 部長・局長	g. 履歴書	h. 広報・広報活動
i. 続ける・貫き通す	j. 小冊子	k. ついに	l. （必然的に）〜を伴う

First Viewing ⟨1'35"⟩

Watch the video and see what the job of a PR specialist is like.

Are you interested in this profession? Choose your answer.

1. very much   2. a little   3. not much   4. not at all

Second Viewing: Watch the video and fill in the blanks.

Director of public relations really entails a lot of different things from dealing with the media that covers the team and (1. _____) and writing press releases to our graphic design and putting together our ticket brochure, and pocket schedules and media guide, you know, different publications like that.

The beautiful thing about this job is there's never (2. _____) or a typical work week. Well, a day in October is different than a day in March. A game day is a lot different than a non-game day. And each game day is totally different because (3. _____) and different events going on here.

So that's... one of the things that I really love about this job is that no two days are ever the same. It varies by season, by what's going on, and it always (4. _____).

I think the internships that I've done were extremely critical in that it actually gives skills and things to put on a résumé. (5.   ). You probably have to start off with, you know, unpaid or very low-paid internships and volunteer work just (6.   ).

It's really just doing whatever you can to get going and sticking with it. And eventually your hard work will pay off, and (7.   ).

<224 Words>

Notes

press release 企業や機関が報道機関向けに発表する広報資料　**pocket schedule** 携帯用スケジュール表
get going 始める、行なう、急いで行く　**pay off** 報われる

Third Viewing: Watch the DVD and take notes.

The main responsibilities of a PR specialist
_____
_____
_____

What this person likes about his/her job
_____
_____
_____

Ways to prepare yourself for this job
_____
_____
_____

Advice to those who want to get into this field
_____
_____
_____

Comprehension

Write *T* if the following statement is true, and *F* if it is false.

1. One part of a PR Director's job involves writing press releases and organizing press conferences. (   )
2. The promotions for the games during the season vary day by day. (   )
3. Having different schedules in spring and fall makes the job difficult for me. (   )
4. Internships are important in that you learn how to write a résumé on the job. (   )
5. According to the speaker, you need to keep in mind that hard work will not always pay off or lead you to the job you want. (   )

Summary & Shadowing Practice

Listen to the CD and fill in the blanks. Then, practice shadowing what you hear.

Bill Cook works as a director of public relations for a baseball team. His main job is (1. _____) with the media, arranging press conferences and other public relations jobs such as (2. _____) ticket brochures and schedules. He really likes his job because there are many (3. _____) events and each game day is very different. He believes that his participation in internship programs taught him some necessary skills to put on his (4. _____) and this helped him to get (5. _____). He thinks that it is important to find something that you really want to do and keep working at it. Usually, hard work will help you get the job you want.

Sentence Structure

Choose the word that best completes the sentence.

1. The job of director of public relations _____ a lot of different things from dealing with the media and arranging press conferences to checking the graphic design.
   a. entail   b. entails   c. entailing   d. entailment

2. I think the internships I've done were extremely critical _____ that they actually give skills and things to put on a résumé.
   a. on   b. above   c. for   d. in

3. It's really just doing whatever you can to get going and _____ with it and eventually your hard work will pay off.
   a. stick   b. to stick   c. sticking   d. stuck

Speaking Practice

Practice the following conversation between a PR director and his assistant. Then, change the underlined words and create your own dialogues.

W: You have a press conference scheduled for <u>this afternoon</u>.
M: Okay. How long will it last?
W: About 1 hour <u>beginning at 3:00</u>. I have materials ready for you.
M: Got it. Thanks. I'm going to mainly talk about <u>our new stadium</u> and <u>its facilities</u>.

Research & Presentation

Use the internet to research some unique PR activities a company, an NPO, or a city has implemented and prepare a short presentation on their features.

Career Tips

✦ 広報担当者 ✦

　広報の仕事は普通、社内向けと社外向けに分けられます。社内では一般に社内報を作成して、社内各部署の動きや状況を共有したり会社案内を編集したりしますが、その際には、各部署と連携を取って情報を共有発信していく必要があります。
　一方、社外向けの場合は、企業理念や活動に関する情報を新聞や雑誌、HPに掲載したり、新商品やサービスの発表などを行いますが、報道関係者に対して行う公式発表の原稿などを作成編集する作業もあります。また、広報部では、リコールや不測の事故を受けての謝罪会見など、危機管理分野における対応も要求されます。
　広報部署における取扱業務は多岐におよびますが、メディアの多様化に伴い、今後はソーシャルメディア関連分野における業務が増える傾向があります。会社やスポーツチームの広報の場合は、チームの認知度やブランドイメージの向上を促進する重要な役割も果たします。情報収集力と高いコミュニケーション力、文書校正力が要求される仕事です。

Unit 2: Advertising Sales Agent

広告代理人

広告代理店の主な仕事は、商品やサービス、あるいは企業の宣伝をすることにありますが、仕事は多岐にわたります。クライアントのニーズや要求に合った宣伝方法を提示、作成するためにはどのような工夫が必要で、また、どのような態度で顧客に接することが大切であるか、Jody Mayo 氏に仕事の内容と持ち備えておくべき資質について聞いてみましょう。

Vocabulary: Match the following English with its Japanese definition.

1. chaotic （　　）
2. client （　　）
3. president （　　）
4. quality （　　）
5. frustrating （　　）
6. concept （　　）
7. environment （　　）
8. appealing （　　）
9. liaison （　　）
10. opportunity （　　）

a. 概念	b. 成長する	c. 顧客	d. 社長
e. 心に訴える	f. 連携	g. いらだたしい	h. 代理店
i. 混沌とした	j. 機会	k. 資質・素質	l. 環境

First Viewing 〈1'54"〉

Watch the video and see what the job of an advertising sales agent is like.

Are you interested in this profession? Choose your answer.

1. very much　　2. a little　　3. not much　　4. not at all

Second Viewing: Watch the video and fill in the blanks.

A typical day at an ad agency is quite varied and usually quite chaotic, but I thrive on that myself. (1. _____) – always exciting. It's definitely not a nine-to-five job. At least, for myself, it's not.

I'm typically dealing with my clients a lot in the evening because they're business owners themselves or presidents or, you know, high level executives, marketing executives, and quite often (2. _____) at night, sometimes on the weekends.

I think the most important quality a person in this industry should have is the ability to listen – listen to their clients, (3. _____), what they want from you. I really feel it is the number one, you know, the most important thing at least I've found over my years of doing this.

You definitely need to have energy, be creative, (4.   ).
It can get frustrating at times because clients change their minds and, you know, you might spend weeks putting together a marketing plan and concepts and then they decide to (5.   ).

Internship is a great…is a great way for a student to get some experience in the agency environment and see what line of work in an agency that is most appealing to them.

Typically in an agency, you know, you would start out (6.   ) where you would, you know, work as a liaison between the client and the agency and manage the account, the day-to-day activities of the account with the client.

It's a very exciting field. You'll never be bored. *There's a lot of opportunities. As I said, on any given day I'm working with, you know, a couple dozen different clients (7.   ). And it's exciting. It's never dull. It's a lot of fun, and I love it. <312 Words>

Notes

thrive on 〜で成長する　**a nine to five job** 定時（9時から5時）の仕事　**at least** 少なくとも
executive 執行役員、経営幹部、重役　**at times** 時々　**line of work** 業種、職種、仕事の流れ
account 営業、業務、取引先、顧客
*There's の後に複数形の名詞が来ているので、文法的には There are が正しい。

Third Viewing: Watch the DVD and take notes.

The main responsibilities of an advertising sales agent

Personality traits and skills necessary for this job

Challenges this person has at work

Ways to prepare yourself for this job

What this person likes about his/her job

Comprehension

Write *T* if the following statement is true, and *F* if it is false.

1. Work at an ad agency can be long and tiring, but it is pretty much routine work. (   )
2. It is not uncommon that business owners and executives call the advertising sales agent at night or on weekends. (   )
3. The most important quality a person in the ad industry needs to have is the ability to persuade the clients to follow regulations. (   )
4. An advertising sales agent needs to have a lot of patience since the clients may change their minds and directions halfway through the project. (   )
5. A person entering an ad agency would initially work as a liaison between the client and the ad agency. (   )

Summary & Shadowing Practice

Listen to the CD and fill in the blanks. Then, practice shadowing what you hear.

Jody Mayo is an advertising sales agent working at an ad (1.   ).
She finds her job very exciting because she doesn't work a typical schedule and she gets to meet different kinds of people in planning their (2.   ) campaigns. Jody believes that (3.   ), patience, energy and listening skills are important in her job so she can better understand the client's (4.   ) and present their ideas in the advertisements. She (5.   ) students to seek out internships as a way to enter the field of advertising.

Sentence Structure

Choose the one underlined word or phrase that must be changed in order for the sentence to be correct.

1. A job at an ad agency is <u>quite</u> varied and <u>usual</u> chaotic, <u>but</u> I thrive <u>on</u> that
                                      A   B   C   D
    myself.

2. I think the most important <u>quality</u> a person in this industry should have is <u>the</u>
                                  A   B
    ability to listen to their clients and understand <u>how</u> their client's <u>needs</u> are.
                                                                        C   D

3. It can get <u>frustrated</u> at <u>times</u> because after you spend weeks <u>putting</u> together a
                    A   B   C
    marketing plan, clients may change their minds and decide <u>to go</u> in a
                                                                                                   D
    completely different direction.

Speaking Practice

Practice the following conversation <u>between employees at an ad agency</u>.
Then, change the underlined words and create your own dialogues.

> *W:* We've been asked to create an ad campaign for <u>a new smart phone</u>, which will be released in <u>6 months</u>.
> *M:* What is unique about <u>this phone</u>?
> *W:* It comes in <u>many different colors</u> and it has <u>a lot of new functions</u>.
> *M:* I think we should highlight <u>all the different colors</u>.

Research & Presentation

Use the internet to research some advertisements (TV commercials) you like and prepare a short presentation on their features.

Career Tips

◆ 広告販売代理人 ◆

　広告には新聞や雑誌などのグラフィック広告、販売促進ツールとしてのカタログやPOP（point of purchase）広告、あるいはWebサイトに掲載するバナー広告、そしてラジオやTVのCMなどがあり、さまざまな媒体を通して商品やサービスの宣伝が繰り広げられます。

　広告代理店では、得意先の要望にあった広告戦略を立案してプレゼンし、案が採択されると、クライアントと製作担当者やメディア担当者と会議を積み重ね、広告やCMの完成までさまざまな調整を行っていきます。

　広告の全体像をクリエイティブディレクターが決め、広告表現をコピーライターが作成し、そしてビジュアルや音楽はそれぞれ映像や音響担当者が協力して作業を行います。独創的な発想力と概念の構築や洞察力が要求されます。

　広告代理店の仕事は、広告作成に至るまで、予算配分やスケジュール管理、品質管理などプロジェクトを総括する仕事を担うため、仕事においてはタフな精神力と体力、柔軟性と調整力、気配りなどが必要になります。

Unit 3 Merchandise Manager

商品マネージャー

商品マネージャーの仕事は、さまざまな商品を買い付けて管理を行うと同時に、商品を店頭に陳列し、消費者に提供する仕事です。商品が雑貨や洋服の場合、世界のユニークな生活雑貨や最新のファッション情報を収集することはもとより、お客が実際にどのような雑貨や服・アクセサリーを求めているかを知らなければなりません。商品や服に関するセンス、そして、店内における接客も大切になります。商品仕入れ部長のJill Bruce 氏に彼女の仕事の内容を聞いてみましょう。

Vocabulary: Match the following English with its Japanese definition.

1. merchandise   (   )   6. place   (   )
2. primary   (   )   7. position   (   )
3. decision   (   )   8. necessarily   (   )
4. corporation   (   )   9. turnover   (   )
5. ultimately   (   )   10. upcoming   (   )

a. 分野	b. 配置する	c. 会社・法人	d. 最終的・究極的に
e. 商品	f. 回転	g. 管理職の	h. 決断・決心
i. 主たる・第一の	j. 地位・職	k. 来たるべき	l. 必ず・必然的に

First Viewing ⟨1'28"⟩

Watch the video and see what the job of a merchandise manager is like.

Are you interested in this profession? Choose your answer.
1. very much   2. a little   3. not much   4. not at all

Second Viewing: Watch the video and fill in the blanks.

A merchandise manager's primary focus in their job is to make the decisions on what merchandise comes into our corporation and ultimately into our stores. A merchandise manager would also have (1.) where the product is placed in our stores, as well as seasonally what would come into our stores, whether or not (2.), or new colors for that season.

The best situation to come into any new position in a corporation would be to have an internship. It's always best to start from the bottom and work your way up. So, if you can hold an internship, you would have a good opportunity to start at the bottom level and (3.).

My words of wisdom for someone who wants to get into merchandising would be (4.) when you don't necessarily have the position that you are looking to have right from the beginning. It's hard to have a position like this. And, it's important to remember that there's a lot of steps that it will take to get to an executive position.

I think it's very important that you choose a career that makes you happy. You should (5.   ) and excited to go to work.

In merchandising there is a constant turnover of new products and new people. So, it's exciting (6.   ). There are also different places all around the world you can travel to, to experience new products for the upcoming seasons. So, (7.   ). It's about the experiences that you can have in this kind of field.

<296 Words>

Notes

as well as 〜と同じように、〜はもちろん　**whether or not** 〜かどうか、いずれにせよ
start from the bottom 底辺から始める、下積みからはい上がる
work your way up 努力で登りつめる、苦労して出世する　**words of wisdom** 名言、格言
right from the beginning 最初から、はなから

Third Viewing: Watch the DVD and take notes.

The main responsibilities of a merchandise manager

Ways to prepare yourself for this job

Advice to those who want to get into this field

What this person likes about his/her job

Comprehension

Write *T* if the following statement is true, and *F* if it is false.

1. A merchandise manager makes purchasing decisions based on the season. ( )
2. A merchandise manager's main responsibility is to promote new products to the media. ( )
3. An internship will give you an opportunity to work in a position you want from the start. ( )
4. In merchandising, there are a lot of steps you need to take to get to an executive position. ( )
5. There are chances to meet new people and travel to different places in the field of merchandising. ( )

Unit 3 ● Merchandise Manager

Summary & Shadowing Practice

Listen to the CD and fill in the blanks. Then, practice shadowing what you hear.

Jill Bruce is a merchandise manager and is (1. _____) for deciding which products will be sold in the stores she works for. She thinks that working in (2. _____) is an exciting job because people in this field often travel to different places to (3. _____) for new products. Her advice for young people who wish to work in this field is to try and find an (4. _____) and then work your way up through the company. Jill thinks it takes a lot of time to become a (5. _____) merchandise manager, but if a person follows the correct steps, they will be rewarded with an exciting career.

Sentence Structure

Put the words in parenthesis in correct order.

1. 私は店内における商品の配置決定の仕事を任されています。

    I have the (determining, of, where, placed, responsibility, product, the, is) in the store.

    _____

2. 自分が幸せを感じるキャリアを選ぶことがとても重要です。

    It's very (career, you, to, feel, that, important, the, happy, choose, makes).

    It's very_____

3. 仕事を通して新しいことを経験し、いろいろな人と出会えることは刺激的です。

    It's exciting to (things, different, through, and, people, experience, meet, new) work.

    _____

Speaking Practice

Practice the following conversation <u>between employees at a merchandising store</u>. Then, change the underlined words and create your own dialogues.

> **W:** How many <u>gift bags</u> do we need for <u>the holiday season</u>?
> **M:** We need <u>about 3,000 bags and 4,000 ribbons</u>.
> **W:** All right, Ken. Can you order them from <u>ABC Gift Supplies</u> this afternoon?
> **M:** Sure, I'll place an order and have them shipped <u>by next Friday</u>.

Creative Activity

Cut out/print out two pictures of merchandise you would like to import from overseas and introduce them to your classmate. Another option is to cut out/print out two pictures of merchandise you would like to export from Japan to overseas markets and explain to your classmate the reasons.

Career Tips

◆ マーチャンダイジング・マネージャー ◆

　メーカーで作られた製品を消費者の要求に合わせて適切な数量仕入れ、適切な価格とタイミングで提供する活動をマーチャンダイジングと言います。商品の仕入れや販売を行なうマーチャンダイザーは、バイヤーとも呼ばれ、一般にアパレルメーカーやデパート、ブティック、量販店などに勤務しています。

　顧客が望む商品を揃えるために、国内外を問わずさまざまな商品を仕入れるため、商品やブランド、デザイナーの発掘はもとより、商品の構成計画や販売促進計画を立てる必要があります。また、流行だけではなく適切な価格設定を考えて商品を選定する必要がり、お店の客層や売り上げの傾向を把握し、鋭い観察眼を常に持ちながら仕事に望まなければなりません。

　マネージャーになるためには、商品の販売や営業の経験を積み、顧客の要望を知るだけでなく、販売計画に基づき店舗設計や商品構成、効果的な陳列や展示の仕方について知識とセンスを持って立案しなければなりません。また、店員のマネジメントを行う能力も身につけることが大切です。

Unit 4 Marketing Manager

マーケティングマネージャー

マーケティング部署では、製品やサービスの開発および販売に先駆け、市場調査を実施します。お客の要望や競合他者の状況、今後の展開に関する可能性など、多角的な市場分析に基づき、今後の販売戦略を立案していきます。マーケティングマネージャーはそれらの仕事を総括しますが、ここでは Diana Zanetto 氏に具体的な仕事の内容を話してもらいます。

○ Vocabulary: Match the following English with its Japanese definition.

1. typical   (   )   6. graduate   (   )
2. arena   (   )   7. connection   (   )
3. relationship   (   )   8. competitive   (   )
4. basis   (   )   9. major   (   )
5. absolutely   (   )   10. apply   (   )

a. 基礎・基盤	b. 競技場・領域	c. 専攻	d. 結びつき・人脈
e. 応募する	f. 関係	g. 競争の・競合的な	h. 卒業する
i. 基礎の	j. 典型的な	k. 常に	l. 全く・絶対的に

○ First Viewing 〈1'23"〉

Watch the video and see what the job of a marketing manager is like.

Are you interested in this profession? Choose your answer.
1. very much   2. a little   3. not much   4. not at all

19

Second Viewing: Watch the video and fill in the blanks.

You have to put together a whole marketing mix for your marketing campaign. So it's not just marketing. It's doing sales, it's doing public relations, it's doing all kinds of different things in your promotional mix to sell (1. _____).

Really there's no typical day at the arena. Every day is different, which is kind of a nice thing about working here. Our days are never the same. We're always looking for new partnerships and relationships to sell our events, but every day is different (2. _____).

You definitely have to be a people person. You can't be afraid of talking to people. You can't be afraid to pick up the phone and form a new relationship. (3. _____), especially when dealing with the media and dealing with promoters on a daily basis.

Definitely (4.   ). That's important when writing press releases or media advisories. You never want to get the wrong message out there.

I think an internship absolutely is key. If you haven't done one yet, try and get it in the summer after you graduate, I think. If this is the field you're looking to get into, (5.   ) or some kind of connection.

It's so competitive to get into this field. I would say "(6.   )."

If you have a dream, go for it. I changed majors in college. My advisor told me "You can't do it." He didn't help me get internship in sports. I did it on my own. I applied on my own.

So I would say never give up. Always, you know, (7.   ).

<276 Words>

Notes

a marketing mix マーケティングの活動要素 4P (**Product, Price, Place, Promotion**) を指す。
a promotional mix マーケティング目標を支援する4つのプロモーション：広告、販売（対面販売）、PR、販売促進（製品ディスプレイ、展示会）などを表す。　**kind of**（米口語表現）どちらかと言えば、やや、大体　**a people person** 人と関わることが好きな人　**on a daily basis** 日常的に
media advisory メディアに向けて流す発表や報告（文脈により、注意や勧告を意味する場合がある。）
go for it 頑張って（〜を目指して進んで）

Third Viewing: Watch the DVD and take notes.

The main responsibilities of a marketing manager

_____
_____
_____

What this person likes about his/her job

_____
_____
_____

Personality traits and skills necessary for this job

_____
_____
_____

Advice to those who want to get into this field

_____
_____
_____

Comprehension

Write *T* if the following statement is true, and *F* if it is false.

1. The speaker first felt excited about doing all kinds of things at work, but now she feels tired of the various chores she has to do. (   )
2. A marketing manager needs to be sociable and good at building new relationships with people. (   )
3. The speaker feels interpersonal communication skills are required but writing skills are not necessary in the field of marketing. (   )
4. According to the speaker, the best way to get into marketing is to take as many marketing classes as you can in college. (   )
5. The speaker's advisor at college did not help her get an internship in sports. (   )

Summary & Shadowing Practice

Listen to the CD and fill in the blanks. Then, practice shadowing what you hear.

Diane Zanetto is a marketing manager. In her job she often mixes together the work of (1. _____), public relations, promotion and other jobs to put together a successful marketing (2. _____) for her clients. Diane believes that people who work in marketing should have good writing (3. _____), and enjoy talking to people and forming new (4. _____) in order to get the job done. It is important to be able to communicate the client's wishes exactly. The field is very (5. _____) and Diane's advice for students is to apply for internships to make the necessary connections.

Sentence Structure

Choose the word that best completes the sentence.

1. Every day is different _____ on what event is coming up.
    a. depend   b. depends   c. to depend   d. depending

2. You can't be afraid of talking to people and forming new _____.
    a. relation   b. relations   c. relationship   d. relationships

3. He didn't help me get an internship in sports, so I _____ for it on my own.
    a. apply   b. applied   c. applying   d. application

Speaking Practice

Practice the following conversation <u>between the Marketing manager and her staff</u>. Then, change the underlined words and create your own dialogues.

> **W:** Our new marketing campaign for <u>the business suits</u> last year wasn't successful.
> **M:** What was wrong with it?
> **W:** Our message missed the target customers, who were <u>business men in their 20s</u>.
> **M:** I see. We should <u>think of some new messages</u> and <u>try them out</u>.

Role Play Interview

You are a reporter and you are going to interview a marketing manager. Ask him/her about their plan for marketing a new smart phone overseas (e.g special features, price, style, brand image, the target customers, etc).

Career Tips

◆ マーケティングマネージャー ◆

　マーケティングとは、新規あるいは既存の製品やサービスの販売促進のために市場調査を行い、市場分析や競合他者の状況を分析しながら、自社の製品企画や販売戦略を立案することを言います。社内にマーケティング部署を持っている企業と、外部の専門会社に委託する企業があります。社内では、営業や販売の現場を経験した者がマーケティング部門に配属される場合が多々ありますが、それは、現場を知らないと戦略を立てることが困難だからです。

　市場調査結果の分析を踏まえ、他の部署（経営戦略本部、営業企画部、販売企画部など）と協力しながら、新製品の生産やターゲットとするユーザーの絞り込み、新規市場での展開方法、販売戦略、宣伝方法などを検討します。そのためには、情報収集や分析力だけでなく、多様な人と協力して仕事を行う必要があります。

　また、実際に全国の販売店や工場などを回って現場の声を聞く必要もあるため、関連部署へのコンサルティングを行なうと同時に、さまざまな問題解決に向けて、自ら積極的に動ける行動力を持ち合わせることが大切です。

Unit 5 Office Manager

オフィスマネージャー

オフィスマネージャーは、会社における事務の仕事を総括する役割を担います。そのため、会社の業務を熟知して仕事の流れを把握し、多様な人々と一緒に仕事をしていく必要があります。Brenda Minella 氏に仕事のやりがいと仕事をしていく上での苦労、そして大切な心がけについて聞いてみましょう。

Vocabulary: Match the following English with its Japanese definition.

1. administration ( )
2. regarding ( )
3. organization ( )
4. motivation ( )
5. concern(s) ( )
6. proficient ( )
7. require ( )
8. shadow ( )
9. clerical ( )
10. rewarding ( )

a. 関心事・懸念	b. 熟達した・堪能な	c. 付き添う	d. 事務管理
e. 雇う	f. 〜に関して	g. 要求する	h. 動機・動機付け
i. 組織	j. 提案する	k. 事務の・書記の	l. 報いのある

First Viewing ⟨2'32"⟩

Watch the video and see what the job of an office manager is like.

Are you interested in this profession? Choose your answer.
1. very much   2. a little   3. not much   4. not at all

Second Viewing: Watch the video and fill in the blanks.

An office manager is responsible for the administration of the office, so that has to do with everything regarding filing or phones, customer service - that kind of thing.
And it also has to do with the people skills that are (1.   ).

It's fun. It can be challenging; it depends on, you know, the kinds of people that you get, but it's very challenging and very interesting because you have different personalities and you try and get this person to work with that person and you find out (2.   ) and what makes them want to work and what makes them want to work better.

I enjoyed it when I was an office manager because I was... I liked being a part of the organization on the management level. I would hear what was going on. I would understand the motivations of the upper echelon as well as *working... and be able to pass that along to the workers, and then take the workers' views and be able to pass that on to the upper echelon. (3.   ).

Well, I was very fortunate that I worked well with the person who was over me and I was... I felt free to explain the concerns that were in the office and I am a "big picture" person so it was easy for me to be able to see this... the point of view of management as well as (4.   ).

26

What I found was... that's really... the challenge of the position is to be able to find ways (5.   ), help people know themselves well enough to find ways to be able to work with other people.

I would recommend an office manager job to someone who is proficient in office skills but (6.   ), somebody who can really see the big picture and know more than what one particular job is required to do.

I guess the best thing would be to intern, shadow an office manager, get experience in the office doing different kinds of clerical work or office work, and you know, you can go from there.

I would say "go for it." It's really an exciting job. (7.   ) and it can be very rewarding. <387 Words>

Notes

be responsible for 〜に責任を持つ、責任を負う　**has to do with** 〜と関係がある
what is going on 何が起こっているか、起こっていること　**upper echelon(s)** 上層部
feel free to 遠慮なく
*working ここで話者は working と述べているが、文法的には the motivations of workers が入り、「上層部と社員の気持ち（動機・やる気・欲求）両方を理解する」という意味になる。

Third Viewing: Watch the DVD and take notes.

The main responsibilities of an office manager

Challenges this person has at work

What this person likes about his/her job

Personality traits and skills necessary for this job

Ways to prepare yourself for this job

Comprehension

Write *T* if the following statement is true, and *F* if it is false.

1. The office manager does not usually answer phones or make phone calls herself since the secretary takes care of that. (　　)
2. It is both challenging and interesting for an office manager to help people with different personalities work together. (　　)
3. As an office manager, it is important to understand the views of both senior managers and the staff. (　　)
4. An office manager does not necessarily need to see the big picture as long as he or she has great office management skills. (　　)
5. In order to have experience in office work and office management, you should do an internship and shadow an office manager. (　　)

Summary & Shadowing Practice

Listen to the CD and fill in the blanks. Then, practice shadowing what you hear.

As an office manager Brenda Minella has to do various types of jobs. She really enjoys working with the (1. _____) people in the office and helping them to work better together. In Brenda's job, she is often the liaison between the workers and (2. _____), and she thinks she is good at this position because she is able to see the "big picture" and communicate (3. _____) with all kinds of staff. Brenda feels that not only (4. _____) skills are very important for her job, but also management skills and (5. _____) skills are important, too.

Sentence Structure

Choose the one underlined word or phrase that must be changed in order for the sentence to be correct.

1. An office manager is responsible <u>for</u> the administration of the office, so that
                                                     A

   <u>has</u> to do with <u>filing</u>, making phone calls, and <u>offer</u> customer service.
    B   C   D

2. I was very <u>fortunately</u> that I worked well with <u>the</u> person who was <u>over</u> me
                 A   B   C

   and I felt free to explain the <u>concerns</u> people had in the office.
                                       D

3. I would recommend an office manager's job to <u>someone</u> who is <u>proficiency</u>
                                                             A   B

   in office <u>skills</u> and who also has a bigger <u>concept</u> of the business.
            C   D

Speaking Practice 🎧 11

Practice the following conversation <u>between a client and an office assistant</u>. Then, change the underlined words and create your own dialogues.

> **W:** Hello. This is <u>ABC company, sales department</u>. Susan speaking.
> **M:** Hello, this is <u>Peter Robinson</u> from <u>Ex company</u>. I'd like to speak with a <u>sales representative</u>, please.
> **W:** I'm sorry all the representatives <u>are out of the office</u>. May I have your number so someone can call you back?
> **M:** Yes, my number is <u>333-2222</u>. Thank you.

Role Play Interview

You are a reporter and you are going to interview an office manager. Ask him/her about the important qualities business leaders should have.

Career Tips

✦ オフィスマネージャー ✦

　企画、営業、経理、人事、総務部など、どのような部署にも事務的な仕事はありますが、事務の仕事を管理するのがオフィスマネージャー（事務局長）の仕事です。会社におけるさまざまな事務処理を円滑に行うため、会社の運営方針に基づき事務手続きを効率化したり、さまざまな事務仕事を振り分けて部下に指示を与えたりする必要があります。そのため、会社の業務に精通し、全体像を把握して仕事の流し方をよく知っている人でなくてはなりません。

　仕事をする上で、誰もが身につけなくてはならない能力の一つは事務処理能力ですが、文書作成能力や効率的なファイリングの方法、PCスキル（ワード文書作成やエクセルの表作成など）は必要不可欠です。

　オフィスマネージャーとしては、それらの技能に加えて、一度にいくつもの事務案件を処理したり、文書作成をしながら同時にスタッフへの指示を出すなど、複数の仕事を同時にこなす平行処理能力を持ち合わせることが重要になります。

Unit 6: Sports and Fitness Manager

スポーツ・フィットネスマネージャー

スポーツ・フィットネスマネージャーは、スポーツクラブの運営に関わる仕事全般に携わります。ジムでは、エクササイズをする利用客は、単独あるいは他の人と一緒に運動をし、心地よい時間を過ごすことができるよう、さまざまなサービスを提供します。ここでは Carlos Tejada 氏に、彼の仕事の内容を詳しく聞いてみましょう。

○ Vocabulary: Match the following English with its Japanese definition.

1. aspect   (　　)   6. swipe   (　　)
2. hire   (　　)   7. customer   (　　)
3. supervisor   (　　)   8. healthy   (　　)
4. issue   (　　)   9. inspire   (　　)
5. concentrate   (　　)   10. innovate   (　　)

a. 集中する	b. 説得する	c. 顧客	d. 問題点
e. 革新する	f. 側面	g. 管理者・監督者	h. 読み取り機に通す
i. 不満	j. 健康な	k. 鼓舞する	l. 雇う

○ First Viewing 〈2'20"〉

Watch the video and see what the job of a sports and fitness manager is like.

Are you interested in this profession? Choose your answer.
　　1. very much　　2. a little　　3. not much　　4. not at all

Second Viewing: Watch the video and fill in the blanks.

The fitness manager is responsible for every single aspect that's going on in the business, in the gym, in your gym. What we're in charge is control…controlling what is in the four walls, meaning (1.), all your operational tasks, sales, vending, personal trainers, staff.

So when I look to hire all the managers or supervisors, I'm looking for people that really enjoy being in the health club. I look for (2.), the attitude that's gonna bring to every day.

This business changes throughout the hours. (3.). Different members, every single member have a different issue. And here what we're trying to do is to open the door for them (4.) and concentrate on their health for the 45 minutes, half hour, or an hour that they're gonna be here. When you're in the fitness environment, you're here to help people.

Unit 6 ● Sports and Fitness Manager

And it's easy just (5.
                    ), trying to get your feet wet, trying to work in the front desk, helping the customer *service coming in, swiping their card, just everyday routine that every customer comes in when they're gonna work out. I mean, I think you start getting a feeling of what this business is all about.

If you're willing to (6.   ), what I would say is…just try it, see how you like it. Get the feeling of working out and trying to be healthier for yourself first and then you're going to inspire other people to do the same thing.

I recommend for people to come into this business. The bottom line is every day you're gonna get a challenge and you've got to keep innovating your structure of work and your program to keep it fresh and keep it fresh enough for people to want more and more and more. And that's always going to be a challenge for you (7.
                    ), as a manager, as a professional. <328 Words>

Notes

be in charge 担当している、〜係の   **operational task** 執行業務   **vending**（自動販売機での）商品販売
throughout hours 四六時中、いつも   **get your feet wet** 新しい事を始める、試す
work out エクササイズをする   **get a feeling of** 〜が分かる気がする、感じがする
what ~ is all about 〜の本質、最も肝心なところ   **be willing to** 進んでする、〜するのを厭わない
The bottom line 肝心な点、要点
＊ここは文法上は **helping the customer coming in at the customer service** となり、「カスタマーサービス（受付）でジムに入って来るお客のサポートをする」の意味と考えられる。

33

Third Viewing: Watch the DVD and take notes.

The main responsibilities of a sports & fitness manager

Personality traits and skills necessary for this job

Challenges this person has at work

Ways to prepare yourself for this job

Advice to those who want to get into this field

Comprehension

Write *T* if the following statement is true, and *F* if it is false.

1. According to the speaker, the fitness manager is usually not involved with sales or other operational tasks. (   )
2. The speaker looks for managers who have energy and enjoy working in a health club. (   )
3. The fitness manager tries to create a space where customers can focus on their health regardless of the problems they have. (   )
4. The speaker's advice, "get your feet wet" means "put your feet in the water before you start swimming." (   )
5. It is not recommended to innovate your program often at the health club since customers can't keep up with frequent changes. (   )

Unit 6 ● Sports and Fitness Manager

Summary & Shadowing Practice

Listen to the CD and fill in the blanks. Then, practice shadowing what you hear.

Carlos Tejada is a sports and fitness manager who manages the business of a sports gym. In his job, he is responsible for the (1.   ), sales, customer service, personal trainers and staff. The job changes (2.   ) the day because members are always coming and going and the manager often needs to deal with each member's requests or (3.   ). Carlos believes this is a good job for people who enjoy (4.   ) service, want to be healthy, and don't mind working long hours. It's a (5.   ) but rewarding job.

Sentence Structure

Put the words in parenthesis in correct order.

1. フィットネスマネージャーはジムで起こっているすべての面において責任があります。
 The fitness manager is (going, single, on, aspect, is, for, every, responsible, that) in the gym.

 _____.

2. ヘルスクラブにいることを本当に楽しむ人を探しています。
 I'm looking (club, in, enjoy, really, health, being, a, people, for, who).

 _____.

3. 私にとって人としてそしてプロとして成長し続けることが課題となります。
 It's always going to be a (growing, me, person, for, a, to, keep, as, and, challenge) as a professional.

 _____.

35

Speaking Practice

Practice the following conversation <u>between a fitness instructor and her manager</u>. Then, change the underlined words and create your own dialogues.

> **W:** You're scheduled to teach <u>two yoga classes</u> on <u>Monday evenings</u>. Is that too much?
> **M:** Are the classes back to back, or is there a break between them?
> **W:** There is a <u>30-minute break</u> between the two classes.
> **M:** <u>That's not a problem</u>. I can teach both classes.

Research & Presentation

You are a reporter and you are going to interview a sports and fitness manager. Ask him/her about the new exercise trends, as well as some popular exercise programs they offer at their gym.

Career Tips

◆ スポーツ・フィットネスマネージャー ◆

　健康志向が高まる今日、人々はそれぞれ自分の体力と好みに合わせてエクササイズを行なっています。ウォーキングをしたり、スポーツジムに通いながらエアロビクスや水泳、ヨガ、筋肉トレーニングなどに励んでいる人もいます。アメリカでは民間のスポーツクラブ数は3万弱あり、日本でも3500以上のクラブがあると言われています。そのように多くのスポーツクラブが存在する中、各クラブはいろいろな工夫を凝らしてプログラムを提供しています。

　フィットネスインストラクターやトレーナーになるためには、さまざまな方法があります。学生の頃からスポーツクラブでアルバイトをして人脈を作る。卒業後フィットネスクラブの運営会社に就職し、社内研修を受ける。あるいは、フィットネス関連会社の主催するフィットネスインストラクター・トレーナー養成コースを終了する。健康・体力づくり事業財団などが行っている資格認定試験に合格する。フリーでオーディションに参加するなど。

　一方、フィットネスマネージャーは、健康作りの良きアドバイザーとしてだけではなく、施設管理責任者として、利用客とのコミュニケーションを取りながら、プログラムの充実を図り、新規会員を獲得してクラブを運営していかなければなりません。

Unit 7　Fashion Designer

ファッションデザイナー

ファッションデザイナーの仕事は一見華やかに見えますが、自分のブランドを持ち、ファッションショーのランウェイに出て脚光を浴びるデザイナーはごく一握りです。多くは、アパレル企業で働いたり、ブティックなどを経営しながら、デザインの仕事に携わる場合が一般的です。ファッションデザイナーになるためには、どのような資質を持つ必要があるのでしょうか。Ricky Lorenza 氏にファッションデザイナーに必要な知識や技能について語ってもらいます。

Vocabulary: Match the following English with its Japanese definition.

1. showcase (　　)　　6. transform (　　)
2. personality (　　)　　7. identify (　　)
3. trait (　　)　　8. contact (　　)
4. creativity (　　)　　9. drawing (　　)
5. abstract (　　)　　10. continue (　　)

a. 創造性・独創力	b. 続ける	c. 試着する	d. 変容させる
e. 連絡をとる	f. 特性・特徴	g. 披露・展示する	h. 確認する・明らかにする
i. 抽象的な	j. 素描・デッサン	k. 販売する	l. 個性・人柄

First Viewing 〈1'43"〉

Watch the video and see what the job of a fashion designer is like.

Are you interested in this profession? Choose your answer.

1. very much　　2. a little　　3. not much　　4. not at all

Second Viewing: Watch the video and fill in the blanks.

A fashion designer has many responsibilities but their main goal is to design clothes for every season of the year. And the way we do this is by designing something we call a collection. A fashion designer showcases their work by putting on a runway show. We use a runway show (1.   ).

The personality traits that make me successful are being creative and with creativity (2.   ). It's very important in this field to be a hard worker because if you don't get anything done, you won't design a thing.

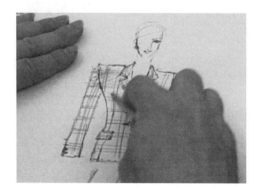

A fashion designer is taking an abstract idea, putting it onto paper, and transforming it into clothing. (3.   ), but if you're hard working and have vision, then you can do this.

Some ways to get experience in fashion design are you can shadow someone by identifying a fashion designer in your area and contacting them by making sure that you can spend time with them to see how they are and (4.   ).

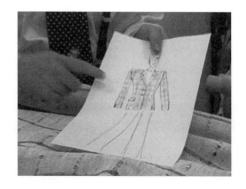

Unit 7 ● Fashion Designer

Other ways to get experience are by going to school. And there are many two-year programs where you can learn how to be a fashion designer. Another good thing to do is (5.   ). And what you do there is you learn what the fashion designer does day in, day out.

So if you think you want to do this, just take a class. In your high school if you have a class like a clothing class, take a clothing class. If you have a drawing class, take that and these classes will (6.   ). So if you know you want to do this, then take a two-year program. It'll definitely help you out. You'll get better experience about what you want to do when you get out into the real world.

I really enjoy being a fashion designer because (7.   ). And when I see people in the street wearing my clothes, it inspires me to make more. So I think I want to continue this throughout my life. <358 Words>

Notes

runway ファッションショーでモデルが歩く舞台・ステージ
put on a runway show ファッションショーを開催する
make sure 必ず〜してください、〜を確認してください　**day in, day out** 明けても暮れても、毎日毎日
take a class クラスを取る、履修する　**see...~ing** …が〜するのを見る　**throughout my life** 一生涯

Third Viewing: Watch the DVD and take notes.

The main responsibilities of a fashion designer

Personality traits and skills necessary for this job

Ways to prepare yourself for this job

What this person likes about his/her job

Comprehension

Write *T* if the following statement is true, and *F* if it is false.

1. According to the interview, a fashion designer usually designs new collections of clothes every six months. ( )
2. It is challenging for a fashion designer to turn an abstract idea into clothing. ( )
3. Shadowing a fashion designer is a good way to experience the job of a fashion designer. ( )
4. It is recommended in the interview that you should take a sewing class at school before you become a fashion designer. ( )
5. The fashion designer interviewed feels most rewarded when he sees some famous people wearing her clothes. ( )

Unit 7 ● Fashion Designer

Summary & Shadowing Practice

Listen to the CD and fill in the blanks. Then, practice shadowing what you hear.

Ricky Lorenza is a fashion designer who designs (1. _____) for the different seasons of the year. Using his creativity and hard work, Ricky (2. _____) his ideas on paper before actually making the clothes for the (3. _____). Ricky believes that in order to become a fashion designer, people can go to school, (4. _____) a designer, or find an internship in the fashion business. He also recommends taking drawing classes in school to build up experience. Ricky's job is very creative and he is (5. _____) when he sees people wearing his clothes.

Sentence Structure

Choose the word that best completes the sentence.

1. The personality traits that make you _____ are being creative and hard working.
       a. success   b. succeeded   c. successfully   d. successful

2. I enjoy being a fashion designer because it lets me _____ my creativity.
       a. express   b. to express   c. expressing   d. expression

3. Seeing somebody wearing my clothes inspires me _____ more clothes.
       a. produce   b. to produce   c. producing   d. production

Speaking Practice

Practice the following conversation <u>between a customer and a sales clerk at a boutique</u>. Then, change the underlined words and create your own dialogues.

> *M:* <u>Hello</u>. Are you looking for anything in particular today?
> *W:* Yes, I'd like to see your <u>new line of dresses</u>.
> *M:* Of course. We have <u>10 new designs</u> this year. Would you like to try some on?
> *W:* Yes, I'd like to try <u>this black dress</u> first.

Creative Activity

Cut out/print out four fashion pictures from a magazine/website and present your favorite and least favorite to your partner. Describe what you like and don't like about the style of clothes. Also, do a makeover of your classmate's fashion. Take a picture of before and after fashion and critique them.

Career Tips

✦ ファッションデザイナー ✦

　ファッションデザイナーは、ファッションを通じて自分の個性や創造性を表現できる仕事ですが、常にセンスを磨き、最新のトレンドを先取りして掴んでおく必要があります。一般には、国内外の服飾専門学校で洋服のパターンやデザインの基礎を学び、アパレル企業のデザイナーとして働く場合がほとんどです。

　ファッション業界では、「ファッションデザイナー」の存在が大切なのはもちろん、市場のニーズを調査し商品企画を行う「アパレル企画担当者」や、ブランドの広告やカタログ作成、ショーや展示会の開催を手がける「ブランド広報担当者」など、多くの関係者が共に連携を取りながら最新のファッションを提供していく必要があります。

　また、ファッションデザイナーとしての経験を積み、将来自らのブランドを立ち上げるためには、デザインだけではなく経営知識も必要になります。

Recreation Worker

レクリエーションワーカー

レクリエーションインストラクターは、レクリエーションを通してさまざまな人との触れ合いの機会を提供すると同時に、健康作りのお手伝いもします。Diana Clauss 氏は大学の教職員を対象にしたレクリエーション活動をしていますが、この分野で仕事をするには、どのような経験を積めばよいかアドバイスしてくれます。

Vocabulary: Match the following English with its Japanese definition.

1. provide   (   )   6. administrator   (   )
2. reduce   (   )   7. officiate   (   )
3. outgoing   (   )   8. assistantship   (   )
4. constituent   (   )   9. expand   (   )
5. faculty   (   )   10. intramural   (   )

a. 学内の・区域内の	b. 助手職	c. 准教授	d. 学長
e. 拡大する	f. 提供する	g. 審判をつとめる	h. 減らす
i. 社交的・外交的な	j. 構成要素	k. 管理者	l. 学部・教授団

First Viewing ⟨2'05"⟩

Watch the video and see what the job of a recreation worker is like.

Are you interested in this profession? Choose your answer.
1. very much   2. a little   3. not much   4. not at all

Second Viewing: Watch the video and fill in the blanks.

The responsibilities of my job entail providing recreational activities for students and faculty and staff on campus. In general, a person that (1.   ) at a university level programs for the student body, and faculty, and staff on campus, providing them with recreational outlets to reduce stress, *to give them some healthy tips, and *provide some healthy habits.

I would say that (2.   ) for someone in my position are really… really easygoing, the ability to roll with the punches, outgoing as well. You have to work with a broad constituent of people here at the university. You work with students, you work with faculty and staff, you work with other administrators, so you really have to be able to mesh within a group setting. *A good team leader…because (3.   ). So I'd say that those are probably the personality traits that one would require.

Some first steps to take to get involved in the recreation field would be to just start officiating some…some leagues in your area – (4.   ) or a baseball league. Start getting some experience working with people who are participating in a recreational league.

And then you're going to want to maybe look to get a graduate assistantship when you are in university or in college. And then you can continue to expand on that, ah… that basis that you've set up as an intramural official, intramural supervisor, and then (5.   ).

My words of wisdom to any student that is looking to get into this field is get as involved as you can… as possible. Start taking a look at some of the universities in your area that you might be interested in. See (6.   ).

Jump on some websites, see what they have, the things that you might be interested in. And start contacting folks in that recreation department to see if they do have student jobs on campus, to see (7.   ), things of the like that will get you a good foot in the door.

<342 Words>

Notes

outlet(s) はけ口　**healthy tips** 健康に関するアドバイス
roll with the punches（困難や問題に）柔軟に対処する　**mesh** 調和する、上手く合う（合わせる）
get involved in 〜に関与する、〜に関わるようになる、一端を担うようになる
participate in 〜に参加する　**jump on** 〜に飛びつく　**things of the like** 同じようなこと
get your foot in the door（目的に向かって）最初の一歩を踏み出す
*to give と *provide の主語はどちらも a person…（3人称単数）となるため、文法的にはそれぞれ gives と provides になる箇所である。
* ここでは a good team leader の前に You have to be が省略されている。

Third Viewing: Watch the DVD and take notes.

The main responsibilities of a recreation worker

_____

_____

Personality traits and skills necessary for this job

_____

_____

Ways to prepare yourself for this job

_____

_____

Advice to those who want to get into this field

_____

_____

Comprehension

Write *T* if the following statement is true, and *F* if it is false.

1. The speaker's job provides recreational activities for people working in the public service and business industries. (   )
2. Recreation workers are not allowed to give tips on how to stay physically healthy. (   )
3. As a recreation worker, you need to be easygoing and sociable as well as to lead a wide range of people in the organization. (   )
4. To start working for a sports league as a referee is one of the first steps you can take to get experience working in the recreation field. (   )
5. An intramural supervisor is someone who oversees an annual professional basketball tournament. (   )

Unit 8 ● Recreation Worker

◯ Summary & Shadowing Practice

Listen to the CD and fill in the blanks. Then, practice shadowing what you hear.

Diane Clauss is a university recreation worker who organizes recreational (1. _____) for students, faculty and staff. Through the recreation activities she supervises, participants (2. _____) stress and become healthy. Her job requires her to work with different types of people and age groups, so she thinks that recreation workers should be very easygoing, (3. _____) and also outgoing. For people who want to do this type of job, Diane recommends that they begin by getting (4. _____) with local sports leagues, and then try to apply for (5. _____) at the university level. She really thinks that getting involved with the local and university sports programs is the best way to start out.

◯ Sentence Structure

Choose the one underlined word or phrase that must be changed in order for the sentence to be correct.

1. The responsibilities of my job entail <u>provide</u> recreational <u>activities</u> for students,
                                            A   B

   <u>faculty</u>, and staff <u>on</u> campus.
     C   D

2. A person who works in a recreation department <u>offers</u> employees
                                                          A

   recreational <u>outlets</u> to reduce their <u>stresses</u> and to give them some healthy
                B   C

   <u>tips</u>.
   D

3. You need to see <u>if</u> they have student jobs <u>at</u> school or student internships that
                  A   B

   will get your <u>feet</u> in the <u>door</u>.
              C   D

47

Speaking Practice

Practice the following conversation <u>between a customer and a recreation worker</u>. Then, change the underlined words and create your own dialogues.

> **W:** On the cruise ship, we will have <u>many different kinds of recreation activities for adults</u>.
> **M:** That sounds great. What kind of <u>activities</u> are available?
> **W:** Well, let's see. There will <u>be dancing, a table tennis tournament, a painting class, a cooking class and so on</u>.
> **M:** Wow. There are so <u>many interesting activities to do</u>.

Research & Presentation

Use the internet to research some recreation activities you would like to introduce to your workplace or organization and prepare a short presentation on their features.

Career Tips

◆ レクリエーションワーカー ◆

　レクリエーション公認指導者あるいは担当者は、レクリエーションを通して、地域市民や職場の人々の触れ合いを深める仕事を支援します。仕事の種類により、レクリエーションインストラクターとコーディネイターの職種があります。日本では、財団法人日本レクリエーション協会が公認する資格を取得する必要がありますが、協会が認可した専門学校、短大、あるいは大学の教育課程を修了すると資格が得られます。

　インストラクターは、年齢に関わらずレクリエーションを楽しみながら健康作りを促進し、さまざまな人々との親睦交流を深めるためのプログラムを提供します。一方、コーディネーターは、レクリエーション活動を推進するプログラムを企画提案したり、必要な人材や団体組織作りを支援します。どちらも、レクリエーション活動を通して、楽しみながら職場での交流、あるいは地域の活性化に貢献する仕事です。自らさまざまなスポーツが好きで、スポーツの楽しさを伝えていくことが大切です。

　レクリエーションはストレスの発散をする場にもなりますので、人々が笑顔でイベントに参加できるよう、人を和ます雰囲気作りが大切になります。また、多様な人々を対象にする仕事であるため、年齢を問わずいろいろな人とコミュニケーションがとれる積極性と社交性が要求されます。

Unit 9　Pre-School Teacher

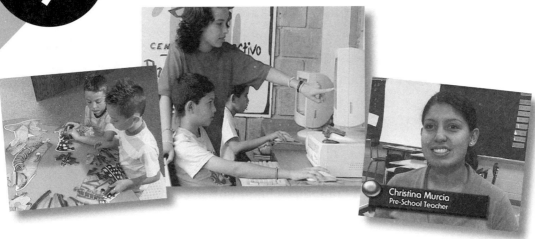

保育園教諭

アメリカでは小学校に入る前の学校（保育園）を一般に Pre-school（プレスクール）、Day Care あるいは Nursery School と言い、数ヶ月の乳児から受け入れてくれる園が多くあります。また、小学校に入る前の 1 年間、幼児は Kindergarten（幼稚園）に入り、集団生活や遊戯だけでなく勉強も習い始めます。Christina Murcia 先生にプレスクールでの仕事の様子と子供達に関して聞いてみましょう。

Vocabulary: Match the following English with its Japanese definition.

1. pre-school　　　（　　）　　6. beneficial　　　（　　）
2. curriculum　　　（　　）　　7. peer　　　　　　（　　）
3. cooperative　　（　　）　　8. shared　　　　　（　　）
4. capable　　　　（　　）　　9. progression　　（　　）
5. rely　　　　　　（　　）　　10. energetic　　　（　　）

a. 精力的な	b. 同僚・仲間	c. 保育園	d. 信頼する・頼りにする
e. 好奇心のある	f. 共有した	g. 教育課程	h. 有能な、実力のある
i. 宿題	j. 進歩・発達	k. 協力的な	l. 有益な

First Viewing 〈2'00"〉

Watch the video and see what the job of a pre-school teacher is like.

　　Are you interested in this profession? Choose your answer.
　　　　1. very much　　2. a little　　3. not much　　4. not at all

Second Viewing: Watch the video and fill in the blanks.

Teaching pre-school is just like teaching everything else. I need to make sure I'm prepared for the day. I need to do lesson plans that follow the curriculum. It's important (1.   ) for the students. And I need to really make sure that I plan those each day.

I think I'm very outgoing. I think that's important because I'm in front of a group of students every day. It's also important that you're cooperative because many times (2.   ).

Teaching pre-school, like I said, is just like everything else, so it's an all-day job. I'm with the kids from the early morning until the afternoon. But uh, I'm with them all day. You know, you have a lunch, you need to (3.   ), and you get to know them – not only as a student what they're capable of in school, but also as people. And you're with them so often during the day, more so than they're even with their parents during the school year. So they really rely on you, and it's important that you are…you're there for them.

Teaching is a lot of at-home work and you need to make sure that you're organized (4.   ) so you're doing less at home. But it could be work at home as well.

Unit 9 ● Pre-School Teacher

I think experience is always important. So I think (5.   ) that's going to give you more experience towards teaching is going to be beneficial. I think it's important to make sure that you're getting a lot of experience before you get into it. So if you want to work at a camp or work at an after-school program or maybe get a job at a school, I think it's also important that you work carefully with, or closely with your peers while you're in college. And, you know, learn from your shared experiences.

Teaching is (6.   ). I love watching the progression of the kids throughout the year, from the beginning when they're shy until the end when they've really opened up. And it's a very rewarding job.

I would recommend this career path to someone who is energetic, outgoing, hardworking, and who really likes to (7.   ) because you never know who's going to come in your class.

<379 Words>

Notes

just like everything else（口語表現）何事もそうですが、他と同じように
at-home work 家でする仕事　**after-school program** 課外（放課後の）プログラム

Third Viewing: Watch the DVD and take notes.

The main responsibilities of a pre-school teacher

Personality traits and skills necessary for this job

Unique features of a pre-school teacher's job

Ways to prepare yourself for this job

What this person likes about his/her job

Advice/recommendations to those who want to get into this field

Comprehension

Write *T* if the following statement is true, and *F* if it is false.

1. A pre-school teacher's job is totally different from teaching in higher education since the children come from different backgrounds. (   )
2. You need to be outgoing and cooperative when you deal with students and other professionals. (   )
3. Pre-school students may spend more time with the teachers than with their parents during a school year, so teachers need to be available and trustworthy. (   )
4. The speaker advises pre-school teachers to bring all the work back home so that they can prepare for classes the next day. (   )
5. It is rewarding as a pre-school teacher to see how children progress throughout the year. (   )

Summary & Shadowing Practice

Listen to the CD and fill in the blanks. Then, practice shadowing what you hear.

Christina Murcia is a pre-school teacher who works with young students every day. She thinks it is important to be very organized in her planning and (1.), so students can understand clearly what she is doing in class. She (2.) all day with her students, so she must be (3.) for many different kinds of activities. Christina thinks that experience in teaching is very important, so students should try to get as much experience as possible while still in (4.). She believes that good teachers have a lot of (5.), like to work hard and enjoy working with different kinds of people.

Sentence Structure

Put the words in parenthesis in correct order.

1. 教師として、教える全てのクラスに役に立つ教材を準備する必要がある。
   As a teacher, I need to (materials, for, the, prepare, all, useful, classes, teaching) I teach.

2. 大学では友達と仲良く緊密に接し、さまざまな経験から学ぶべきです。
   You should work (peers, while, closely, your, in, learn, college, you're, and, with) from various experiences.

3. 私はこのキャリアをエネルギッシュで、異なるタイプの人と一緒にやっていくのが好きな人に薦めます。
   I would recommend this career to someone who is energetic and (types, along, to, get, different, likes, of, who, people, with).

Speaking Practice

Practice the following conversation <u>between a teacher and a student</u>. Then, change the underlined words and create your own dialogues.

> W: Mr. Peters. What are we going to do <u>on our class trip</u>?
> M: Well, we're going to visit the <u>City Museum</u> and then <u>watch a play</u>.
> W: <u>What play</u> are we going to watch?
> M: We are going to see "<u>The New Team</u>." I'm sure <u>you'll enjoy it</u>.

Creative Activity

You are an elementary school teacher. Create two different types of overnight school trips and show the parents those plans with pictures of different locations, activities, hotels, etc. The parents will make a final decision on the destination based on the information they get from the teacher.

Career Tips

✦ 保育園・幼稚園教諭 ✦

　日本では、幼稚園は文部科学省管轄で幼児教育を施す学校として、一方、保育園は厚生労働省管轄で乳幼児から小学校入学前の子供を預かる福祉施設として分類されています。それぞれ、保育士あるいは幼稚園教員養成過程を持つ専門学校か短大、大学で課程を修了するか、国家試験に合格すると免許がもらえます。

　保育園では０歳児から保育しますが、幼稚園では普通３歳児からの子供を受け入れ、３歳児は「年少」、４歳児「年中」、５歳児「年長」と呼び分けています。子供の年齢に応じてクラス分け、遊びや運動、音楽などを通じて子供達の健康と人間関係、言葉や表現力などを育んでいきます。個性豊かな子供達の成長を見守ると同時に、集団生活における協調性や規律なども身につけることができるよう、暖かく指導することが求められています。

　保育士や幼稚園教諭は、朝夕幼児の送り迎えをする保護者へのあいさつ、遊具の点検や連絡帳の記入、部屋の壁面の飾り付けや教材準備、保育の記録、行事の打ち合わせや準備、職員会議など、さまざまな仕事をこなしていかなければなりません。時には子供達の喧嘩の仲裁に入ったり、怪我の応急処置なども行います。従って、幼児への暖かい眼差しはもちろんのこと、情熱と体力、保護者とのコミュニケーション、そしてさまざまな問題に対処していく柔軟な姿勢も大切になります。

Unit 10 Hotel Manager

ホテルマネージャー

ホテルには通常、客室・レストラン・会議場または宴会場などの部門があります。各部署に責任者がいますが、全ての部署を総括する立場にある人をマネージャー（支配人）と言います。ここでは支配人である Jeff Plamondon 氏に、日々の業務と仕事に必要な資質について聞き、また、どのようなバックグランドや経験を持つ人がホテルで働いているかを語ってもらいます。

Vocabulary: Match the following English with its Japanese definition.

1. associate   (   )   6. banquet   (   )
2. satisfaction   (   )   7. luncheon   (   )
3. profit   (   )   8. culinary   (   )
4. specifically   (   )   9. degree   (   )
5. housekeeping   (   )   10. limitless   (   )

a. 犠牲	b. 調理・料理の	c. 業界・産業	d. 限りない
e. 利益	f. 仕事仲間	g. 学位	h. 客室清掃係
i. 宴会	j. 満足	k. 昼食	l. 特に・とりわけ

First Viewing ⟨1'37"⟩

Watch the video and see what the job of a hotel manager is like.

Are you interested in this profession? Choose your answer.

1. very much   2. a little   3. not much   4. not at all

Second Viewing: Watch the video and fill in the blanks.

It's all about the customers and the associates. So (1. _____). Associate satisfaction, guest satisfaction, sales and profit – what's important is to concentrate on all four.

You need to be able to communicate with people that work with you, your customers, and then those that are above you. You also have to be a motivator. (2. _____) because your day is never… it's not the same, which is a great thing if that's what you're interested in.

Typically, the day will start …we'll do a meeting in the morning (3. _____) that are working that day to talk about specifically that day. We'll spend day time with the associates whether it's in housekeeping, walking the floors, the kitchen.

Lunchtime, I'm (4. _____). Whether it be a banquet luncheon or a restaurant luncheon, I will be there to keep an eye on what's going on.

Unit 10 ● Hotel Manager

A typical day… I'll have a couple of guest issues and (5.   ) that'll crop up. You may have some weeks that are very busy. And it may be a 50-hour work week, sometimes more… *depends on what's going on. And then there may be weeks where it may be a little less.

A number of the associates or managers that work at the hotel do have hotel degrees, culinary degrees, and a number of them don't. They may have a liberal arts degree. They may (6.

).

We have about 50% of our managers (7.   ).
It truly is an industry that if you work hard and you're able to work with other people in teams and in groups, your future is limitless. <287 Words>

Notes

motivator やる気を引き起こす人、意欲を高める人（要因）、動機付け　**whether...or** …かどうか
keep an eye on 〜から目を離さない、注意を払って見る　**crop up** 突然現れる、生じる、持ち上がる
liberal arts 人文科学、教養課程
***depends on** 「〜によりけり」は、書き言葉の場合、**It depends on~** と主語を入れるのが普通だが、口語では主語を省略して使用する場合がある。

Third Viewing: Watch the DVD and take notes.

The main responsibilities of a hotel manager

Personality traits and skills necessary for this job

Challenges this person has at work

Backgrounds of hotel employees

Advice to those who want to get into this field

Comprehension

Write *T* if the following statement is true, and *F* if it is false.

1. Hotel managers are concerned about not only sales and profits but also about the satisfaction of guests and associates. ( )
2. Managers and supervisors have weekly meetings and discuss issues and events happening at the hotel. ( )
3. Managers at a hotel need to spend time with the staff and oversee all operations. ( )
4. According to the speaker, a hotel manager always works at least 50 hours a week. ( )
5. You are required to have a degree in the hotel business in order to become a good hotel manager. ( )

Summary & Shadowing Practice

Listen to the CD and fill in the blanks. Then, practice shadowing what you hear.

Jeff Plamondon works as a hotel manager and has to supervise a (1. _____) of jobs each day. He believes it is very important to be a good communicator and (2. _____) in order to provide customer service. On a typical day, Jeff will attend meetings with staff and (3. _____), listen to guests, check in on the different floors, visit the hotel kitchen and (4. _____) hotel events. Each day is different and the hours worked each day also vary. Some hotel managers studied the hotel industry in university, but many began working at lower (5. _____) in the hotel and worked their way to management level jobs.

Sentence Structure

Choose the word that best completes the sentence.

1. Flexibility is _____ because your day is never the same.
      a. required   b. requiring   c. require   d. requirement

2. You should pursue _____ you are interested in.
      a. wherever   b. whenever   c. whatever   d. however

3. Whether it be a banquet luncheon or a restaurant luncheon, I will be there to keep an eye _____ what's going on.
      a. in   b. for   c. with   d. on

Speaking Practice

Practice the following conversation <u>between a customer and a receptionist at a hotel</u>. Then, change the underlined words and create your own dialogues.

> *W:* Hello. This is the Royal Hotel. May I help you?
> *M:* Yes, I'd like to make a reservation <u>for next Tuesday for two people</u>.
> *W:* Yes, we have a <u>double room</u> available. Smoking or non-smoking?
> *M:* Non-smoking, please. And I'd like to have a room with an ocean view, if possible.

Role Play Interview

You are a reporter and you are going to interview a hotel manager. Ask him/her about the luxury services they offer at their 5-star hotel.

Career Tips

◆ ホテルマネージャー ◆

　ホテルは、利用客に宿泊のスペースを提供するだけでなく、レストランや宴会、会議の場を用意します。接客業が主な仕事ではありますが、接客以外にも企画や営業、マネジメントの仕事があります。

　マネージャーになるためには、いろいろな部署での経験を重ねて管理職につく場合と、他のホテルやサービス業における管理職経験者が、ヘッドハントされて職に就く場合があります。マネージャーは、ホテルの施設や設備の確認やサービスのチェック、経営状態の把握をしておく必要があります。また一般の利用客に対しても現場で接する機会がありますが、得意客や角界の著名人が利用する場合などは直接挨拶に伺う場合もあります。従って、おもてなしの心と正しいマナーで相手に接することが要求されます。

　また、最近は世界有数のホテルが日本にも参入してきており、日本のホテルでもそうですが、外資系のホテルでは特に、世界中からの宿泊客に対応するため、英語によるコミュニケーション力が求められます。

Unit 11　Interior Designer

インテリアデザイナー

インテリアデザイナーは、依頼主の要望に合わせてさまざまな空間をデザインして提供します。Chasity Manning 氏から、インテリアデザイナーがどのようにしてクライアントと接し、デザインを手がけていくのか、そして快適な空間をデザインしていく上で大切なことがらは何かを聞いていきましょう。

Vocabulary: Match the following English with its Japanese definition.

1. individual　　（　　）　　6. include　　（　　）
2. scheme　　　（　　）　　7. dedicated　（　　）
3. particular　　（　　）　　8. versatile　（　　）
4. furniture　　（　　）　　9. extremely　（　　）
5. contractor　　（　　）　　10. worthwhile（　　）

a. 献身的な・熱心な	b. とても・極めて	c. やりがい・価値のある	d. 視覚の
e. 含む、含める	f. 個人の	g. 契約者・請負人	h. 創立者
i. 家具	j. 概要・計画	k. 多才の・融通のきく	l. 特定の

First Viewing ⟨2'25"⟩

Watch the video and see what the job of an interior designer is like.

Are you interested in this profession? Choose your answer.
1. very much　　2. a little　　3. not much　　4. not at all

Second Viewing: Watch the video and fill in the blanks.

An interior designer takes the artistic ideas of an individual and they make *it come to be within some sort of setting. Whether it be a room, a doctor's office, or an apartment building, they basically (1.).

The main thing they need to do is actually listen to what the client wants. That's the key in the position. They basically take everything that the client wants – the client has a vision for what they see, whether it be color schemes or particular furniture that they may want. And they basically take all the information the client gives them and create basically a plan for (2.).

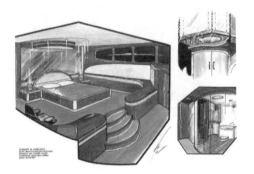

It all starts with organization. They have to put everything out on paper. And with it being on paper they are able to show the contractors exactly what they want. And (3.) that are included within this field, they're able to show the contractor what the space is to look like. And the contractor can take all the information that the interior designer gives them and is able to actually carry out those plans.

The AutoCAD software is a software that you use to basically create the vision that you have for the room you're designing, and you're able to see it ahead of time before you actually put any work into the room. So you'll be able to see (4.) and you'll be able to understand what will work and what won't work.

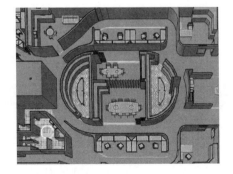

Unit 11 ● Interior Designer

First and foremost, an interior designer should (5.   ) – those are the two main aspects to interior design. You also need to be hard working, of course, and you need to be willing to be very dedicated to your position because it is a lot of work.

When you're going into the field of interior design, you need experience because without experience you won't get very far. And the only way to do that is to have internships, and internships help build experience. So you should try to get one or two, even three internships with different companies. So it shows that you're versatile and that (6.   ) within the field.

I would recommend this position to someone who is extremely creative. The position at the end of the day....you need to be creative to do this position and to hold this job. And without creativity in this position, you won't be as successful.

I definitely say the sky's the limit. (7.   ). Don't let anyone stop you from reaching those goals of being an interior designer. It's a hard position but it's definitely worthwhile if you put in the hard work and the time and dedication to the position. <460 Words>

Notes

sort of は **kind of** と同じように口語表現で、「どちらかと言えば、やや、大体」を意味する。
carry out 実施・実行する **CAD** は **Computer Aided Design** の略で、コンピュータ支援設計。 **Auto-CAD software** はオートデスク社が開発した 3D で立体的な図面描画が可能な汎用の CAD ソフトウェア。建築、インテリア・土木・機械分野などで多く利用されている。 **ahead of time** 前もって、事前に
First and foremost なによりもまず、真っ先に **won't get very far** あまりうまくいかない、成功しない、出世しない、行詰まる。 **at the end of the day** 一日の終わりに、結局最後は、要するに
The sky's the limit. 可能性は無限だ、不可能はない。 **stop ...from ~ing** …が～をするのを妨げる
*the artistic ideas は複数形なので、文法的には it ではなく them が使われるところである。

Third Viewing: Watch the DVD and take notes.

The main responsibilities of an interior designer

Features of special software interior designers use

Personality traits and skills necessary for this job

Ways to prepare yourself for this job

Advice to those who want to get into this field

Comprehension

Write *T* if the following statement is true, and *F* if it is false.

1. An interior designer's job is to take the clients' ideas and create the vision for a particular setting. ( )
2. An interior designer is required to give the client instructions on the color schemes of furniture suitable for the space. ( )
3. Interior designers use special software to create the image of the room, which allows the customer to see in advance what design works or not. ( )
4. According to the speaker, qualities interior designers need to have are hard work and dedication as well as artistic creativity. ( )
5. The speaker thinks doing an internship with one company is sufficient to get experience before you go into the interior designing business. ( )

Unit 11 ● Interior Designer

Summary & Shadowing Practice

Listen to the CD and fill in the blanks. Then, practice shadowing what you hear.

Chasity Manning is an interior designer who works with clients to bring their ideas regarding an interior space to reality. She listens to the clients (1. _____) their vision for the space, including (2. _____) and colors and then creates a design using computer software. (3. _____) then use her designs to construct the space. Interior designers should be (4. _____), creative and organized in order to communicate the client's wishes accurately. Chasity believes that experience is the best teacher for this job, and recommends young people to (5. _____) internships in the field in order to get experience.

Sentence Structure

Choose the one underlined word or phrase that must be changed in order for the sentence to be correct.

1. The <u>main</u> thing they <u>actual</u> need to do is to listen to <u>what</u> the client wants and
     A   B   C

   take <u>everything</u> the client requests into consideration.
          D

2. The clients have <u>a</u> vision for what they see, <u>whether</u> it be color <u>schemes</u> or
               A   B   C

   particular <u>furnitures</u> that they may want.
              D

3. You also need to be <u>hard working</u> and be very <u>dedicating</u> to your <u>position</u>
                    A   B   C

   because it is <u>a lot of</u> work.
            D

Speaking Practice

Practice the following conversation <u>between a customer and a sales clerk at a furniture store</u>. Then, change the underlined words and create your own dialogues.

> *W:* I'd like to see <u>your sofas</u>, please.
> *M:* Sure. We have a nice selection <u>on the 2nd floor</u>.
>   Are you interested in <u>leather or</u> cloth?
> *W:* I'm <u>interested in leather</u>.
> *M:* Okay. We are now offering <u>a 20% discount</u> on the sofas with <u>a red tag</u>.

Creative Activity

You are an interior designer and you need to show your customers some sample furniture for their living room. Cut out/print out pictures of different sofas and low tables from a magazine/website and explain about the features and prices. The customers will choose the one they like the best for their home.

Career Tips

◆ インテリアデザイナー ◆

　インテリアデザイナーは、主にインテリアデザインオフィスや家具専門店、あるいは建築事務所に勤務しますが、経験を積んだ後フリーで活躍する場合もあります。仕事の内容としては、個人住宅や店舗を手がける場合と、百貨店や商業施設等を手がける場合がありますが、いずれにせよ、まず依頼主と打ち合わせをして要望を聞き、空間のコンセプトやイメージを固めて行きます。その後、イメージに沿ってデザイン描き、パース（立体的なデザイン）を仕上げます。また、クライアントと相談しながら、部屋の壁や床、家具等の素材や色彩を選び提案します。

　クライアントとの打ち合わせにおいて、インテリアの好みだけではなく、趣味や好きな絵などについても聞き取り、クライアントの嗜好にあった空間作りを提供できるよう高いコミュニケーション力と洞察力が必要になります。デザインに関しては、設計図が描けるよう知識と技能を身につけると同時に専門ソフトを使いこなし、独自のセンスを磨くことも大切になります。経営の面からは、インテリアに関するさまざまな商品知識を持ち、クライアントの予算に合わせて家具や棚などの見積もりを行い、納期までに仕上がるよう、全てのプロセスを管理する力も必要になります。

Unit 12 : Video Editor

映像編集者

映像編集の仕事は、多くの映像を目的に合わせて編集していく根気のいる作業です。ここでは、Monique Guz 氏に実際の仕事の内容と、仕事をする上で必要な能力や技術に関して話してもらいます。彼女がどのようにしてこの仕事に就いたか、また、クリエイティブな仕事をする上でどのような資質が必要かについても語ってもらいます。

Vocabulary: Match the following English with its Japanese definition.

1. manipulate   (   )
2. footage   (   )
3. patience   (   )
4. transition   (   )
5. organized   (   )
6. structure   (   )
7. vocational   (   )
8. predictable   (   )
9. collaborate   (   )
10. likewise   (   )

a. 構造	b. 移行・場面転換	c. 映像画面	d. 協同・恊働する
e. 忍耐	f. 同様に	g. 予想できる	h. きちんとした・整った
i. 技術の	j. 細かい	k. 職業上の	l. 操作する・扱う

First Viewing ⟨2'41"⟩

Watch the video and see what the job of a video editor is like.

Are you interested in this profession? Choose your answer.

1. very much   2. a little   3. not much   4. not at all

Second Viewing: Watch the video and fill in the blanks.

The job of a video editor is to digitize, organize, and manipulate footage for a project. One of the biggest personality characteristics you must have to be a video editor is patience because it's a lot of work and it's a very long process and (1. _____).

Also you need to be very, very organized because *there's so many files – not even just video files, but sound bites and background music and text and graphics and transitions – everything. So you need to be organized.

Another thing is you have to be extremely creative because you really want to make someone interested in what you're doing. So you have to think *what would someone want to see, or what would draw someone into your product or your film project, like, (2. _____).

You really need to take the time to think about what you're doing on the whole scale before you start editing; (3. _____) of what you're doing. Not exactly every little thing, but the overall structure you need to know…and then from there on your creativity takes over.

(4. _____).
If you really want to get into the editing field, you might want to join a club in high school, either at a television station or even just working with media because they all interrelate with each other.

There are vocational schools and technical schools out there. Definitely take a program there. I learned most of what I know from a vocational school and that was a two-year program and I feel that I learned the most there.

Internships are extremely important because not only does it set you up with networking and puts a foot in the door for you, but (5.   ). You learn certain things about the field in your classroom in theory and books, but the real world is a different experience. And you see how things really are these days and it keeps you up to speed with what's the latest trend and what kind of technology they're using now.

Ideally, this job would be great for somebody who wants to come to work every day (6.   ) because it's not a predictable job. Every day is different. You'll get different projects and you'll have different ideas in the works.

It's really rewarding to be able to collaborate with other people who have ideas to express and likewise they learn from you. So at the end of the day, it's very rewarding to know that you have a network of people who are all as creative as you and just having the support of a team.

So if really…this applies to you and you're that person, definitely (7.   ) because you'll just see how one little thing will just lead you to where you feel at home. <482 Words>

Notes

sound bites ニュース番組に挿入される、録画された発言やインタビューから短縮して編集した簡潔な抜粋
on the whole scale 全体的な規模（スケール）で　**take over** 引き継ぐ、支配する
interrelate with each other 相互関係を持つ　**in theory** 理論上は、理論的には
keep you up to speed with what's the latest trend 最新の動向に遅れないようについていく
apply to 当てはまる、適用する　**lead...to~** …を~に導く　**feel at home** 馴染む、くつろいだ気持ちになる
*there's so many files の there's は口語で使うことはあるが、複数名詞が後に続くため文法上には **there are** が正しい。*what would someone want は間接疑問文のため、文法上は語順を変えて **So you have to think what someone would want** （あるいは **like**) **to see** となるところである。

Third Viewing: Watch the DVD and take notes.

The main responsibilities of a video editor

Personality traits and skills necessary for this job

Ways to prepare yourself for this job

Unique features of a video editor's job

What this person likes about his/her job

Comprehension

Write *T* if the following statement is true, and *F* if it is false.

1. A video editor's job is to mostly shoot films of different activities based on the clients' requests. ( )
2. In order to work as a video editor, you need to be patient and very organized since you deal with so many different files. ( )
3. When you edit video footage in a creative way, it is important to be first attentive to small details and later come up with a framework for your project. ( )
4. Internships help you not only experience the real world and learn the latest trends, but also establish your network in the industry. ( )
5. The speaker feels she is competing against other creative professionals on the same team when they work together on a big project. ( )

Summary & Shadowing Practice

Listen to the CD and fill in the blanks. Then, practice shadowing what you hear.

Monique Guz is a video editor who edits video for different (1.   ). She believes that the traits necessary for this job are (2.   ), organization and creativity. Monique believes that vocational and technical schools are a good place to take (3.   ) and training in video editing. Internships are also very important as they can provide real-world experience not found in the classroom. Internships are also a good way to begin (4.   ) a network of people working in the field. Video editing is not a (5.   ) job and most days the work is very different as video editors often work on a variety of video clips.

Sentence Structure

Put the words in parenthesis in correct order.

1. 何があなたの製品に人を引きつけるかを考えなければなりません。
   You have to think (someone, your, would, product, into, draw, what).

2. インターンは、ネットワークを作ってくれるだけでなく、その仕事が実際にどのようなものかを見ることができるので、非常に重要です。
   An internship is extremely important because (it, only, you, set, not, with, networking, does, up), but you actually see what the job is like.

3. 小さな事柄から大きな偉業を達成することができることを知るのは大切なので、できるだけ早く取りかかりなさい。
   Get involved as soon as possible because it's important to (accomplishments, to, you, know, little, will, things, lead, great, how).

Speaking Practice

Practice the following conversation <u>between a video editor and her friend</u>. Then, change the underlined words and create your own dialogues.

> *W:* Hey. Did you see that crazy video about the <u>baby dancing with his pet dog</u>?
> *M:* Yeah. My sister <u>sent me a link</u>.
> *W:* It really <u>made me laugh</u>. It was very funny and it captured a great moment.
> *M:* We should make a video like that with <u>our own dog</u>.

Role Play Interview

You are a reporter and you are going to interview a video editor. Ask him/her about their favorite online video clips.

Career Tips

✦ 映像編集者 ✦

　映像編集は、テレビ番組や映画製作、あるいはインターネットでの動画編集において欠かせない仕事です。通常は、専門学校や大学の映像学部で基礎知識や技能を学んだ後、映像制作会社やテレビ局に就職して、アシスタントとして経験を積み、細かい専門の技術を修得していきます。

　すばらしい番組を企画し製作しても、映像編集が上手くなければ、完成度の高い作品はできません。その意味で映像編集の仕事はとても大切です。シーンに応じて秒単位以下での編集作業が必要になることもあり、職人の技が要求されます。専門のソフトの使い方を熟知しておくことはもちろん、集中力と忍耐力も必要です。

　一つの作品を作り上げるためには、プロデューサーやディレクター等との話し合いは必要不可欠で、制作者の意図を汲取り、要望に合わせた映像編集をしていくためには、自分自身の感性を磨くと同時に、関係者との密なコミュニケーションを取っていくことが重要になります。

　映像編集では、さまざまな資料映像を使います。そのため、世の中の主な動きを捉えて、必要に応じて映像編集を行い、多様な要求に対応できるように備えることも大切です。

Unit 13 Desktop Publishing

オンライン出版

DTP (Desktop Publishing) とは机上・卓上出版のことで、雑誌や新聞、冊子などさまざまな出版物の編集やレイアウトをコンピューターで行っていきます。出版業界もデジタル化が進み、仕事の内容にも変化が起きています。ここでは Bill Greenwood 氏に、DTP の仕事の内容と必要なスキルをどのように獲得していくべきかについて話してもらいます。

Vocabulary: Match the following English with its Japanese definition.

1. copy   (   )   6. varied   (   )
2. specifications (   )   7. content   (   )
3. attentive   (   )   8. feature   (   )
4. detail   (   )   9. ballpark   (   )
5. improve   (   )   10. fulfilling   (   )

a. 球場	b. 仕様書	c. 内容	d. 注意深い
e. 細部・詳細	f. 達成感のある	g. 公園	h. さまざまな・変化のある
i. 特集記事	j. 向上・上達させる	k. 原稿・広告文	l. 大衆雑誌

First Viewing 〈2'29"〉

Watch the video and see what the job of a desktop publisher is like.

Are you interested in this profession? Choose your answer.
1. very much   2. a little   3. not much   4. not at all

Second Viewing: Watch the video and fill in the blanks.

Desktop publisher I think is more along the lines of laying out a newspaper or a magazine or some sort of publication, newsletter or whatever it is that you do. Basically you're in charge of getting copy together, editing that copy, making sure it follows specifications, and then taking it and putting it on the page in a way (1. _____) and make them want to read that.

A lot of it now also has to deal with the internet because that's kind of where all the newspapers and magazines are kind of going these days. (2. _____), putting it up on the internet, doing web design and things like that.

You have to be very attentive to detail, and you have to really know style and grammar. A lot of people don't really have a strong grasp of that when they come into college. But it's something you can learn easily and it's something (3. _____) in everyday life to sort of improve your skills there.

In terms of writing and reporting, (4. _____) and you need to not be scared to talk to people that you don't know and ask them questions that are going to make them feel uncomfortable.

Then in terms of layouts, you just have to have a good eye for what looks good. I would say if you read a lot of magazines and newspapers or go to a lot of websites now... I should also mention (5.   ) for what...for what you like. And that's what I try and do when I design it.

This is definitely not nine to five. (6.

) because my tasks are pretty varied. So one day I could come in and write an article and do an interview and maybe edit a story. And then the next day I'll come in and do some content management, but then maybe call someone real quick and do a quick interview. So you're doing all kinds of stuff.

I think internships are very important for this field because a lot of it has to do with experience. You can (7.   ) and you can know all the rules for writing a news story or a feature or how to do an interview. But when you actually get out there and have to do it, it's a whole *nother ballpark.

This is definitely a very cool industry. If you can get in in the right place, it's going to keep growing and growing especially if you get into it on the internet side. And it's very fulfilling and it can be very exciting. So go for it. <464 Words>

Notes

more along the lines of より〜の線で、より〜のようで　**things like that**（口語表現）そのようなこと
have a strong grasp of 〜をしっかり把握する、十分理解する　**in terms of** 〜に関して、〜の点から
has to do with 〜と関係がある・〜を扱う
***nother** は、口語表現でスラングとして用いられるが、普通、書き言葉では **other** が使われる。
a whole other~ で「全く別の〜」という意味になる。

Third Viewing: Watch the DVD and take notes.

The main responsibilities of a desktop publisher

Personality traits and skills necessary for this job

Unique features of a desktop publishing job

Ways to prepare yourself for this job

Comprehension

Write *T* if the following statement is true, and *F* if it is false.

1. Desktop publishing and other types of publishing are similar in that they both need to follow specifications and draw readers' attention. ( )
2. As newspapers and magazines go online, appropriate content management as well as attractive web design become more indispensable. ( )
3. Nowadays most high school students have a strong grasp of writing style and grammar before they enter college. ( )
4. When you interview people, you need to make sure none of your questions will offend the interviewees. ( )
5. During the internship in the desktop publishing, people learn how to write stories, but not how to interview people. ( )

Summary & Shadowing Practice

Listen to the CD and fill in the blanks. Then, practice shadowing what you hear.

Bill Greenwood is a desktop publisher who organizes copy, which is written content for (1. _____), including magazines, newspapers, newsletters and websites. This job requires Bill to pay (2. _____) to such details as grammar, writing styles, (3. _____) and design. Desktop publishing requires different skills such as interviewing, writing and designing. He also thinks that internships are very important in this type of job because interns can learn the "real world" style of writing, (4. _____) and designing publications. Bill believes that the desktop publishing industry is growing, especially with work (5. _____) to the internet, so it is a very exciting time to join this field.

Sentence Structure

Choose the word that best completes the sentence.

1. You're in charge of getting copy together and putting it on the page in a way that _____ readers to it.
   a. is drawing   b. has drawn   c. will draw   d. will be drawn

2. Don't be scared to talk to people you don't know and ask them questions that are going to make them feel _____ .
   a. uncomfortably   b. uncomfortable
   c. uncomforting   d. uncomforted

3. You may know all the rules for _____ an interview, but when you actually get out there and have to do it, it's a whole other ballpark.
   a. give   b. being given   c. having given   d. giving

Speaking Practice

Practice the following conversation <u>between web designers</u>. Then, change the underlined words and create your own dialogues.

> **W:** We need to lay out the new design for the <u>September</u> issue.
> **M:** How many <u>articles</u> are there?
> **W:** We have <u>14 articles</u> and <u>30 pictures</u>.
> **M:** Okay. Let's begin with <u>page one</u> and see how we do.

Research & Presentation

Use the internet to research some interesting examples of desktop publishing (DTP) and prepare a short presentation on its features.

Career Tips

◆ 出版企画・編集者 ◆

　本や雑誌等の出版の仕事は大きく企画、編集、予算や制作費の管理、営業に分けられます。雑誌の場合、原稿そのものは自社専属のライターが書いたり、外部の執筆者に依頼したりしますが、原稿が入稿されると編集作業に入ります。原稿の校閲を行い、必要に応じて写真撮影を行い、全体のレイアウトが決まったら版下を作り、そして最後に製版印刷にたどりつきます。

　雑誌などの企画では、斬新な発想が求められることがあるため、日頃からいろいろなことに興味を持ち、するどい洞察力を持ちながら情報を収集し、読者の興味ある企画を立案して出版までこぎ着ける実行力が重要になります。また関係各社との連絡を取り合いながらの作業が続くため、さまざまな場面で説得力や交渉力も要求されてきます。

　原稿編集では、手書きの原稿を推敲していく場合もありますが、IT技術が伴うに従い、原稿入稿も編集もパソコンを使いながらの作業が一般的になっています。しかし、文言を校閲する場合には、一語一句隅々まで原稿を読み、内容の確認や「てにおは」のチェックをしていく必要があり、文章力と同時に根気のいる仕事でもあります。出版業界の仕事は華やかに思われることもありますが、実際には地味で粘り強く、注意深く細かい作業を続けていくことが求められます。

Unit 14: Event Planner

イベントプランナー

イベントプランナーはさまざまなイベントを企画し準備運営します。顧客の要望に合わせてスポーツイベントを行ったり、コンサートやセミナー、各種展示会なども開催します。Diane Bozak 氏は多くのイベントを手がけますが、目に見える以外の裏方の仕事も多くあります。イベント企画運営の実際の仕事内容と、大切な心がけについて聞いてみましょう。

Vocabulary: Match the following English with its Japanese definition.

1. oversee   (   )   6. offer   (   )
2. oriented   (   )   7. direction   (   )
3. multiple   (   )   8. glamorous   (   )
4. profession   (   )   9. persistent (   )
5. proposal   (   )   10. related   (   )

a. 根気（粘り）強い	b. 華やかな	c. 指示・方向	d. 職業
e. 監督する	f. 提供する	g. 企画書	h. 〜指向・優先の
i. 関連している	j. 誠実な	k. 自明の	l. 多数の

First Viewing ⟨2'29"⟩

Watch the video and see what the job of an event planner is like.

Are you interested in this profession? Choose your answer.
1. very much   2. a little   3. not much   4. not at all

Second Viewing: Watch the video and fill in the blanks.

An event planner oversees an event. It sounds self-explanatory but they are the ones who oversee an event (1.   ).
They make sure that there is a space for the event. There's all the services you would need for an event – that there's food, that there's audio-visual, that there's parking – anything that goes along with an event happening. That's what they do.

As an event planner you need to be very... a very outgoing person. You need to want to deal with people, be very customer service-oriented. It's a very customer service-focused job. So you also need to be very detail-oriented. You need to (2.   ), you know, multiple tasks all at the same time.

It is not a nine to five job at all. Event planning can be nine to five some days and it can be 7:00 AM to midnight other days. If there's an event going on, you need to be there for the whole event. It could go from 7:00 in the morning until 10:00 at night.

In order to get into the event planner profession I think that shadowing and internships and things like that are a very good idea. I got into this profession (3.   ). And I've had college students who worked for me who've gotten into this profession. So definitely by doing, by finding some way to get involved with someone who already does this*.

In order to get in the event planning field you can (4.   ). You have to be able to write proposals and things like that, so you have to be able to communicate clearly with other people.

80

Unit 14 ● Event Planner

*Any sort of leadership-type class they're offering because you need to be able to work on your own sometimes, and be able to lead other people, and have them follow your direction (5.   ) or things like that.

I think that the position and the job is not always as glamorous as people make it sound out to be. I think a lot of people have this idea – "oh, I want to plan an event, or I want to plan weddings because it sounds like it's so much fun." Not to say that my job isn't fun, there are a lot of days I love my job, but it is also a lot… a lot of work. So I think understanding that there's a lot of work that goes along with the fun – that would be (6.   ).

I think the thing I enjoy most about this line of work is the variety of the types of work I get to do. Every day is not the same. I could come into work one day and be running a soccer camp. I could come into work the next day and be running a memorial service for someone. So it's a very different kind of work and every day is different…every day is different.

If you really want to have a job in event planning, I would say "be persistent." Take the classes that seem to be very well related to what you want to do but be persistent. Look for people (7.   ) or look for positions that… while it's not the glamorous side of things, you'll get the most experience from those jobs. <561 Words>

Notes

self-explanatory 明白な、自明の、分かりやすい　**audio-visual** 視聴覚の
get involved with ～に参加（関与）する　**work on your own** 一人で働く、一人で取り組む
Not to say that（口語表現）～と言うわけではないにしても　**get to do**（口語表現）〈することが〉できる
a memorial service 告別式、追悼式、慰霊祭、法事
*by ~ing の文の後、**you may get into this profession** が省略されている。
*Any の前に **Take** が省略されている。

Third Viewing: Watch the DVD and take notes.

The main responsibilities of an event planner

Personality traits and skills necessary for this job

Ways to prepare yourself for this job

Challenges this person has at work

What this person likes about his/her job

Advice to those who want to get into this field

Comprehension

Write *T* if the following statement is true, and *F* if it is false.

1. An event planner prepares for the event, making sure all the services necessary are provided. ( )
2. As an event planner, you need to be able to pay attention to details and focus on one task at a time. ( )
3. According to the speaker, event planners usually work in the office from nine to five. ( )
4. Taking communication classes and leadership classes will be helpful if you want to become an efficient event planner. ( )
5. The profession of event planner is not necessarily as glamorous as it looks. ( )

Summary & Shadowing Practice 🎧 28

Listen to the CD and fill in the blanks. Then, practice shadowing what you hear.

Diane Bozak works as an event planner and takes care of all the (1. _____) before, during and after an event. She believes an event planner must be an outgoing and (2. _____) person to handle different events at the same time. Diane works long hours to plan events, and her day does not have a (3. _____) schedule. Some days she begins work very early and goes home very late in order to take care of a variety of (4. _____) for a successful event. Diane's advice for people who want to be an event planner is to find an internship where you can work for many different (5. _____).

Sentence Structure

Choose the one underlined word or phrase that must be changed in order for the sentence to be correct.

1. <u>In order to</u> deal <u>with</u> people, you need to be customer-<u>focus</u> as well as detail-
        A   B   C

    <u>oriented</u>.
      D

2. You need to be able to work <u>by</u> yourself and, at the same <u>time</u>, be able to <u>led</u>
                                        A   B   C

    other people and have them <u>follow</u> your direction.
                                   D

3. <u>Although</u> you sometimes <u>get</u> to meet famous people <u>through</u> events, the job is
        A   B   C

    not always as <u>glamor</u> as people make it out to be.
                  D

Speaking Practice 🎧 29

Practice the following conversation <u>between a customer and a wedding planner</u>. Then, change the underlined words and create your own dialogues.

> W: For your wedding, would you like <u>a buffet dinner</u> or <u>table service</u>?
> M: I think we'd like a <u>buffet style party</u>.
> W: Okay. How many <u>guests are you inviting</u>?
> M: We're expecting <u>about 120</u>.

Creative Activity

You are a wedding planner. Create three types of wedding plans and show a potential couple those plans with pictures of different locations, clothes, reception settings, food, etc. The couple will choose one of the wedding plans.

Career Tips

✦ イベントプランナー ✦

　毎日どこかで大小さまざまなイベントが開催されています。イベントはスポーツやコンサートのようにエンターテイメント性のあるものから、商店街や地域での親交を深めるお祭り、新商品の展示会、セミナーや会議など多種多様で、イベントプランナーは主催者側の目的と意向に合わせてイベントを企画して提案します。

　企画が採用されると、具体的な進行スケジュールを組み、必要に応じて司会者やゲストの手配、会場の選定やイベントのパンフレットの製作とプロモーション、そして音響や照明、食べ物などの手配もして、当日のイベント運営を行います。

　イベントプランナーになるためには、特別に求められる資格や学歴はありませんが、まずクライアントと信頼関係を築くことが大事です。そして、論理的な思考と情報の収集、独創的な企画力が大切になります。またイベント運営にあたっては、スケジュール管理、チーム内外との調整や関連部署との交渉力が必要となります。また人を楽しませることが好きで、ユーモアや情熱がある人、トラブルの時にも臨機応変に対応できる柔軟性と問題解決能力を備えている人が求められます。

Unit 15 Photographer

写真家

写真家の仕事は文字通り写真を撮ることですが、雑誌や新聞社に所属して勤務する場合とフリーランスで働く場合があります。Scott Bush 氏は独立して写真スタジオを経営しながらさまざまな写真を撮っていますが、写真撮影の仕事と経営面の話、そして写真家になるために必要な事柄をアドバイスしてもらいましょう。

Vocabulary: Match the following English with its Japanese definition.

1. photography   (   )   6. stagnant   (   )
2. portrait   (   )   7. amazing   (   )
3. document   (   )   8. resources   (   )
4. shoot   (   )   9. mentor   (   )
5. process   (   )   10. admire   (   )

a. 画家	b. 賞賛する	c. 驚くべき	d. 指導者・教育係
e. 許可する	f. 情報供給源	g. (細部を) 記録する	h. 肖像画
i. 写真	j. 停滞した	k. 過程	l. 写真を撮る

First Viewing ⟨2'43"⟩

Watch the video and see what the job of a photographer is like.

Are you interested in this profession? Choose your answer.
1. very much   2. a little   3. not much   4. not at all

Second Viewing: Watch the video and fill in the blanks.

What a photographer does... basically you probably have two parts – the photography end of it and then the business end of it. The photography end of it is pretty self-explanatory. You know, I take pictures.

(1. _____), whether it's weddings or portraits or still life or documenting a football game, things like that, that's pretty much the easy part. The business end is really what takes a lot of work.

A typical work week would be shoots, usually any day or nights, weekends. And then you have the processing of those shoots. I'm all digital so I process (2. _____) and then I usually just get them printed at a lab. There's a lot of business work, you know. Most people...when you think of photography and being a photographer, you don't think about the business end of it, but you actually have to do a lot more business-wise than photography.

I'm my own boss. I have my own company. (3. _____), so you have to be willing to put in the time and the effort to be successful and support your family.

You don't want to get stagnant with your photos or your work, you always want to (4.) or week or every picture you take.

If you're in high school and you want to get started in the field of photography, I would tell you two things. One is… go to the internet. I mean, the internet is amazing with what's out there in terms of resources – what you can learn. (5.

). Find out if it's gonna be sports or weddings or newspaper photojournalism. Find out what you would like to do. And then, the second step would be … find the mentor, someone that you really admire in the field whether it be a veteran professional or even somebody that's just starting.

Personal advice is just never stop shooting. Always (6.
). If you're specializing in working with portraits and weddings, shoot still-life. Shoot, walk down the street and take pictures.

I love being a photographer because I get to experience a lot. I get to experience new places, new people, new cultures, some important moments in peoples' lives and some low points in people's lives. I get to experience (7.
). As a photographer you're there and a part of it. <419 Words>

Notes

takes a lot of work かなりの作業である、やることが沢山ある、結構大変である（口語表現）
business-wise ビジネスの面では、ビジネス的には　**get started**（口語表現）活動し始める
photojournalism 写真を主体とするジャーナリズム・報道活動　**specialize in** 〜を専門にする
still-life 静物、無生物の画題

Third Viewing: Watch the DVD and take notes.

The main responsibilities of a photographer

A typical work week

Things you should keep in mind in this profession

Ways to prepare yourself for this job

Advice to those who want to get into this field

What this person likes about his/her job

Comprehension

Write *T* if the following statement is true, and *F* if it is false.

1. A photographer's job is not limited to taking pictures of many different objects, scenes, and activities. (　　)
2. The photographer interviewed takes both analog and digital pictures. (　　)
3. The speaker runs his own photo studio and supports his family. (　　)
4. Nowadays, you can learn about photography not only from your mentor, but also from the internet. (　　)
5. The only thing the speaker enjoys about being a photographer is experiencing the exciting moments of people in their lives. (　　)

Summary & Shadowing Practice

Listen to the CD and fill in the blanks. Then, practice shadowing what you hear.

Scott Bush is a photographer who owns his own photography business. For his business Scott takes and (1.   ) photos for a variety of events. He has two main jobs, taking pictures and running his (2.   ). As a photographer, Scott works different hours depending on the event. He will often work at night and on weekends if the event (3.   ) it. Besides taking pictures, Scott has to do different tasks in order to successfully conduct his business. His advice to young people who want to be (4.   ) is to continue taking pictures, use the internet to research the profession and find a (5.   ) to teach you the business.

Sentence Structure

Put the words in parenthesis in correct order.

1. あなたは成功し家族を養うために努力を惜しまずに行わなければなりません。

   You have to be willing to (make, your, and, family the, successful, support, effort, be, to).

2. 私の個人的なアドバイスはそれがどのようなものであれ写真を撮るのを止めないということです。

   My personal advice is just (matter, stop, are, what, shooting, never, pictures, no, they).

3. 自分の仕事に行き詰まらないために、あなたはいつも次の段階に自分を押いやらなければなりません。

   In order not to get stagnant with your work, (to, level, yourself, next, push, you, always, should, the).

Speaking Practice 🎧 31

Practice the following conversation <u>between a customer and a photographer</u>. Then, change the underlined words and create your own dialogues.

> **W:** Hi, the photos I took <u>at your wedding</u> are ready.
> **M:** <u>That's great</u>. I'd like to see them so I can order some prints.
> **W:** Yes, of course. Can you come to the studio <u>next Monday around 2 pm</u>?
> **M:** Sure. <u>I can't wait to see the photos</u>.

Research & Presentation

Use the internet to research some interesting, impressive, or outstanding photographs you like and prepare a short presentation on their features.

Career Tips

✦ 写真家 ✦

　写真家には、通信社や新聞社、あるいは出版社に所属して働く専属カメラマンとフリーで活躍しているカメラマンがいます。写真は報道を主とする写真、風景を専門にする写真、結婚式や他の行事を撮影する写真、スタジオで撮る人物や商品の写真など、さまざまなものがあります。写真の種類や発表する媒体により仕事の中身が異なってきます。

　写真業界でもデジタル技術の進歩により、写真家が写真を撮る時にもデジタルカメラを使用することが多く、コンピュータを使っての写真加工や編集、印刷技術を身につける必要があります。このような技術は専門学校や大学の芸術学部でも学ぶこともできますし、プロのカメラマンのアシスタントとして働きながら、さまざまな撮影方法を身につけることもできます。

　しかし、プロの写真家になるためには、カメラの知識や技術の修得だけでは不十分で、例えば、人物の撮影では、被写体をリラックスさせ、自然な表情を引き出せる雰囲気を作る工夫が求められます。また、さまざまな芸術作品を鑑賞したり、他の写真家の作品を参考にしながら、創造的な表現方法を学び、日頃から独自の美的感覚とセンスを磨く必要があります。

TEXT PRODUCTION STAFF

edited by	編集
Eiichi Kanno	菅野 英一
Kenji Matsumoto	松本 健治
English-language editing by	英文校閲
Bill Benfield	ビル・ベンフィールド
cover design by	表紙デザイン
Ruben Frosali	ルーベン・フロサリ

CD PRODUCTION STAFF

recorded by	吹き込み者
Bianca Allen (AmE)	ビアンカ・アレン (アメリカ英語)
Howard Colefield (AmE)	ハワード・コルフィールド (アメリカ英語)

本書にはCD（別売）があります。
1枚組　2,500円（税別）

Career Design on DVD
プロフェッショナルに学ぶキャリアデザイン

2015年1月20日　初版発行
2015年1月31日　第2刷発行

著　者　　塩見 佳代子
　　　　　Angus McGregor
　　　　　滝田 尚広

発 行 者　佐野 英一郎

発 行 所　株式会社 成 美 堂
　　　　　〒101-0052　東京都千代田区神田小川町3-22
　　　　　TEL 03-3291-2261　FAX 03-3293-5490
　　　　　https://www.seibido.co.jp

印 刷・製 本　倉敷印刷株式会社

ISBN 978-4-7919-3390-7　　　　　　　　　　Printed in Japan

・落丁・乱丁本はお取り替えします。
・本書の無断複写は、著作権上の例外を除き著作権侵害となります。

Top Careers in Two Years
英語で学ぶキャリアデザイン入門

●2年ほどの専門教育を必要とする様々な分野の仕事を取り上げ、その第一線で働く人々へのインタビューを含め、その仕事に就くために必要な学習、スキル、資質や適性、仕事の内容、将来の見通しなどを紹介します。

1. Communications and the Arts	第1巻	デジタル時代のアートと情報産業
2. Business, Finance, and Government Administration	第2巻	ビジネス、金融、政府職員
3. Construction and Trades	第3巻	建設と自動車
4. Retail, Marketing, and Sales	第4巻	小売業、マーケティング、販売職
5. Health Care, Medicine, and Science	第5巻	ヘルスケア、医療、サイエンスセクタ
6. Hospitality, Human Services, and Tourism	第6巻	接客業、サービス業、観光
7. Computers and Information Technology	第7巻	コンピュータと情報技術
8. Education and Social Services	第8巻	教育と社会福祉
9. Public Safety, Law, and Security	第9巻	公共の安全性、法と保障
10. Food, Agriculture, and Natural Resources	第10巻	食品、農業、自然資源
11. Manufacturing and Transportation	第11巻	製造と流通

DVD 全11巻　各18-23分　本体価格　¥210,000＋消費税

オリジナル音声英語版　チャプターメニュー＆英語字幕表示機能付き
英文指導者用ガイド（CD-ROM収納）付き
米国 FFH 社国際配給　©2009

＊ ライブラリーユース、クラスルームユース著作権処理済みです。
許諾書発行いたします。

お問い合わせは：
（株）グローバル・リンケージ
TEL：03-5777-0668　FAX：03-5777-0669
info@glinkage.com
URL http://www.glinkage.com

株式会社 グローバル・リンケージ
〒105-0012
東京都港区芝大門2-4-8
メビウスビル3F
Tel. 03-5777-0668　Fax. 03-5777-0669
URL：http://www.glinkage.com

MEMO

MEMO

MEMO

MEMO